CABBAGES
AND KINGS

CABBAGES
AND KINGS

JAMES B. EDWARDS

aventine press

Published by Aventine Press
55 East Emerson St.
Chula Vista CA 91911
www.aventinepress.com

ISBN: 978-1-59330-873-5

Library of Congress Control Number: 2014922509
Library of Congress Cataloging-in-Publication Data
Cabbages and Kings

Printed in the United States of America

CONTENTS

"We are but older children, dear, who fret to find our bedtime near."
Lewis Carroll
Through the Looking-Glass

Let's face it, when an American male reaches the age of 89, and most of his friends are long dead, he has one foot in the grave and the other on a banana peel. So, if he has anything he wants to say, he had better get on with it. For a title, I wanted to use something from the Walrus and Carpenter:

"The time has come, the Walrus said,
To talk of many things:
Of shoes-and ships-and sealing wax-
Of cabbages-and-Kings-"

I'll go with Cabbages and Kings, though I've always loved Whittier's: "Of all sad words of tongue or pen, the saddest of these, *"It might have been."*

The book is mostly about some extraordinary people I've met along life's highway; most are now dead. It should have been written earlier, while they were around to edit and greatly improve it.

I start the book with Rollin Gillespie, because he was the most extraordinary person I have ever met. NASA and ARPA were his ideas. Gillespie was a Tesla-like figure, and like Tesla, he was unappreciated, unsupported, exploited and betrayed.

The chapters that follow are in order of occurrence with portraits of people associated with that particular period. Later in the book, I deviate from this pattern and go random in my stories of interesting people, places, and events.

In the opening section on Rollin Gillespie, I had to cherry-pick from a large stock of his reports and proposals, otherwise this section would have outweighed the Encyclopedia Britannica. Only his career in the aerospace industry is covered. In an attempt to convey the gist of some proposals, only the introductions and illustrative pages are included. All material is unedited and just as Gillespie wrote it.

Rollin W. Gillespie

Rollin W. Gillespie

Rollin Gillespie was the most extraordinary man I have ever known. He was well over six feet tall, raw-boned, square-jawed, slim and wiry – like Gary Cooper – a Plainsman. He always had a big smile and a "hale-fellow" manner. He radiated energy; often working round-the-clock for days on end. He loved to talk on a galaxy of subjects: rocket design, interplanetary trajectories, political systems- "ships and shoes and sealing wax, cabbages and kings."

When Vicki and I would visit Rollin and Helen in McLean, there was a set routine. Helen and Vicki would repair to the kitchen to cook and discuss food and arts and crafts. Rollin and I would make for the living room. I would say: " Well, Rollin, what's new?" For the next hour or so I would bask in a private lesson from a world-class lecturer. I would keep the ball rolling with an occasional: "That's amazing!" or "Really, I didn't know that."

At a 1962 White House NASA Space Council meeting for the Apollo moon landing program, President Kennedy told the NASA attendees to "go round up all the Rollin Gillespies". Gillespie was one of the top pioneer rocket scientists in the world. He was also well known world-class maverick, who got things done in spite of corporate and government bureaucratic interference and heel dragging. A good example would be his March 1958 proposal to the Air Force: A Unitized Rocket. An Advanced Rocket Design and Comprehensive Plan for its Manufacture and Operation.

It would be a five year program; two years to test and finalize the design and build the production facilities. Three years to produce and deliver 675 rockets. The total five year cost of the program would be $235,000,000, yielding a cost of $349,000 per rocket. The three year production run cost would be $250,000 per rocket. The rockets would have a launch weight of 525,000 pounds, and a thrust of 600,000 pounds. They would be capable of delivering a 10,000 pound payload to a range of 8000 miles. They would be capable of reaching any target on earth from the continental United States. Gillespie said: "that the main purpose of the rockets will be to make their own use as a weapon unnecessary".

"The design was originally undertaken with manned space flight in mind. There are many obvious applications for a cheap and reliable rocket already proven out at the expense of the military establishment, which can place a payload of 7600 pounds in a satellite orbit."

Gillespie presented the proposal to the top brass of the Air Force. He finally appeared before the newly formed Senate Space Committee, chaired by Senator "Stu" Symington. After the hearing, Symington invited Gillespie to the Senator's home. They spent the day and much of the night outlining the parameters of a long range defense and space program. Symington said these were the first recommendations he had seen that made sense. At one point, when Rollin was pressing for an early go-ahead, Symington had remarked: "Frankly, Mr. Gillespie, it just doesn't cost enough."
Notwithstanding the "bargain basement" price tag, this meeting ultimately resulted in the establishment of NASA and ARPA/DARPA.

When word got around of Gillespie's "bargain basement" defense and space program, he was ordered to destroy all copies of the proposal. Gillespie enhanced his "maverick" credentials by personally printing 100 copies, which he mailed to top industry and government officials around the country. He saved a few copies and later gave Copy # 9 to me.

Unsung and forgotten pioneers are an old story. D. W. Griffin (movies), Will Durant (autos), Nicola Tesla (electricity). Rollin W. Gillespie is the forgotten man of the space industry. Today, almost no one knows the key role he played in rocketry, NASA, ARPA, and space exploration. There should be a *Gillespie Memorial* in the Air and Space Museum. The opening section (47 pages) of *Cabbages and Kings* are an introduction to his work.

1946-1948 General Electric Company
Served on the five-man steering committee for the Hermes Program, which was responsible for much of the early liquid rocket engine development for the U.S.Army .

Organized and managed the Thumper Project, America's first anti-ballistic-missile (ABM) rocket program. The mission was to detect, intercept and destroy incoming intercontinental ballistic missiles. This was the first of a series of a ABM projects that would evolve into the "Star Wars" program. Rollin obtained a contract at Wright Field to study vibration in the Hermes liquid propellant rockets. This was the first program to study the problem of vibration in liquid rocket motors.

1950-1952 Aerojet
In charge of the high-energy propellant program at the Rocket Physics Lab. Gillespie was the first to recognize the phenomenon of spin vibration in liquid propellant rocket combustion chambers. Nobody had been able to build workable large liquid rocket motors. They vibrated themselves to pieces on the test stand or launch pad. Rollin discovered the problem was "spin vibration" (see Spin Vibration). He developed a solution called the "Gillespie Fix". He applied their findings to the design of a 300 ton thrust chamber for the Bomarc, producing the first successful large liquid rocket motor in the U.S.

1952-1956 Rocketdyre
Rollin was put in charge of the Rocket Engine Advancement Program. He supervised the engineering, testing, and analysis of all combustion devices in the research program. He was project engineer for the 450,000 pound thrust chamber, which was the prototype for the F-1 engine used in the Saturn V Lunar rocket. President Kennedy was able to announce the NASA Apollo moon landing program only because Rocketdyre had already tested several large prototype engines. Rollin was firmly convinced that had he not pioneered the design of the large combustion chamber first at Aerojet and then a Rocketdyre, no one else would have done so in a timely manner. He was thoroughly familiar with what was going on in the rocket development companies across the nation at that time.

1956-1957 Jet Propulsion Lab (JPL)
Gillespie supervised the calculation of the specific impulses of 350
liquid propellant combinations. This reduced the large number of
possible combinations to a few best choices. He supervised the design
and development of the concentric splash plate injector. See The JPL
Injector.

In 1957, while at JPL, Gillespie wrote a letter to President Eisenhower
recommending the creation of a national space agency, and another
agency to take over those rocket programs having military value. The
letter pointed out that the military is incapable of conducting good
research,which the space program and military rockets require. That
research and production lines are incompatible; that the military is in
effect a production line. That to change the military to make it capable
in research would destroy its production-line characteristics, and render
it unfit for waging war. That research be removed from the military and
from its immediate supervision.

The letter was forwarded to the Joint Chiefs of Staff and to Senator Stu
Symington, Chairman of the newly created Senate Space Committee.
After appearing before the Committee, Rollin was invited by Senator
Symington to his home. Rollin spent the day and much of the night
briefing on a future space program. Symington said no one else had
proposed anything closely approaching it in achieving what appeared
to be needed. As a result of this meeting, the Committee set in motion
legislation that created NASA and ARPA. President Eisenhower
established NASA in July 1958; it became operational on October 1,
1958. See Formation of NASA and ARPA.

1958-1963 Lockhead Missiles and Space Co.
Gillespie supervised a crew of 100 who designed the liquid hydrogen-
liquid oxygen rocket that led to the Centaur and Agena space rockets.
After five \months of intensive work on his own time evening and
weekends, Gillespie came up with a "Gillespie Fix" that enabled he and
his colleagues John Breakwell and Stan Ross to solve the previously
insoluble Kepler Problem. They perfected the equations by which
one could select a trajectory which would carry a space craft from

one moving planet to another moving planet. They gave their paper at the 14th Annual Meeting of the American Rocket Society (ARS) in November 1959 in Washington, DC. Blagonrovov, Chief of the Soviet Rocket Program, and his boss, Sedov, President of the Soviet Academy of Science attended the meeting. They bought up the entire stock of preprints, which they published, without permission, within three months in Russia. Immediately afterward they launched the first interplanetary rocket, intended to go to Venus. The next day they announced they had lost contact with it. Later, Gillespie and crew discovered their calculations contained an error – a plus where there should have been a minus. The Russians had launched their Venus rocket on the wrong trajectory. In Typical Russian fashion they had the gall to say it was deliberate, despite the fact that they had used the material without permission. Gillespie initiated and led orbit mechanics studies, culminating in the NASA SP-35 Interplanetary Trajectories Handbook. He directed in-house planetary missions studies that resulted in three original manned planetary contracts funded by NASA , and known as EMPIRE.

1963-1969 Principal Engineer, Missions Planning and Operation, Advanced Manned Missions Program, Headquarters, NASA, Washington, DC.

In November 1962, Gillespie was scheduled to present a paper: "Design of a Chemical Rocket for Manned Interplanetary Expeditions" to the ARS convention in Los Angeles. Wernher Von Braun had the paper canceled. At that time, Von Braun was promoting NOVA, a Saturn C-8 rocket having a thrust of 12,000,000 pounds. Gillespie's single-Stage-to-Orbit propane rocket would have 3.4 times the mass of the NOVA, and would place 3.7 times the mass of cargo on Earth parking orbit. The incident triggered an order by President Kennedy to the NASA Space Council to "bring all those Gillespies into NASA headquarter." Thus, Rollin was drafted by the President to join NASA, which he did in April 1963.

Applying his vast experience in mission planning, space mechanics, launch rocket and space craft propulsion and systems engineering,

Gillespie was made responsible for the development and analysis of trajectories associated with advanced manned missions suitable for a post-Apollo space program. During his tour of duty at NASA, Rollin continued working on his latest version of a comprehensive space exploration program, titled: <u>A Total Unified Plan For Space Research And Solar System Exploration Throughout The Next 35 Years.</u>

In Rollins words:
"Rocketry had reached a point of transition between learning how to design and operate rockets and using rockets as tools for space exploration. It was now possible to specify in detail the propulsion maneuvers for round-trip flyby and landing expeditions to Mars and Venus".

Gillespie proposed that a large single-stage rocket could best meet the requirements of a manned, interplanetary rocket program. It would carry 666 metric tons of cargo to earth-parking orbit. The propane rocket would have a launch mass of 12,000 metric tons, a diameter of 20 meters, and a height of 100 meters. It would utilize pressure stabilized tanks and a plug-nozzle engine. It would be able to return to base and land on its tail. The current issue of Aviation Week & Space Technology (12/16/13) discusses NASA's and DARPA's long range objective of building single-stage-to-orbit rockets able to return to base and land on their tails. Gillespie offered a detailed plan for such a system in 1969.

In a repeat of the 1958 scenario, Rollin was ordered, in writing, by NASA Headquarters to destroy all copies of his new proposal, and to confine his work to the Shuttle. Rollin considered the Shuttle to be a dead end. On the day he received the order, Rollin personally xeroxed 100 copies of the proposal. He distributed 50 copies to the top management of NASA Headquarters, and mailed the rest to individuals all over the country. It was a repeat of 1958. He then waited to be fired; when that did not happen, he retired.

Rollin Gillespie played a key role in the creation of NASA and DARPA. Large rocket engines and interplanetary missions are to a great degree the result of "Gillespie Fixes". Today, NASA aspires to be in perhaps 2030 where they could have been in 1970 had they implemented Gillespie's pioneering proposals. He was truly a remarkable man!

In 1970, Rollin and I finished writing With All Odds Against Us, The Nature and Magnitude of the Soviet Systemic Threat.
Starting in the 1920s and 1930s and continuing until its demise, the Communist Party of the Soviet Union (CPSU) pursued a long-range plan of world conquest:

- To build the most powerful political party and control apparatus in the world—the CPSU and the political police--the NKVD/KGB.
- To build the most powerful industrial machine in the world--a giant arsenal.
- To build the most powerful military machine in the world--the Red Army and Red Air Force.

The book tried to explain the fundamental nature of the system Lenin and Stalin created and to describe the incredible slaughter and suffering it caused. Attention was focused on the vast Gulag and the tens of millions of innocent people who perished in this frozen hell. Writers on Communist exterminations dealt almost exclusively with the millions who died in the Collectivizations and the Purges ; their estimates of the numbers who had died in the Gulag system always appeared to be entirely too low.

Inasmuch as there were literally decades during which tens of millions of people passed through the Gulag system, and all reports of survivors spoke of appalling death rates, it became obvious that the numbers who died in the Gulag, had to be much larger than the combined totals of those who died from other causes. In support of this hypothesis, Rollin and I compiled data on estimated Gulag populations and death rates in various periods. These data were combined with estimated death tolls from other causes, such as the Purges and Collectivization, to arrive at an overall total extermination figure chargeable to the CPSU. The total figure arrived at was approximately 107,000,000. The Soviet Union had been a vast slaughter house—an abattoir.
Utopia Empowered became Murder Incorporated!

Rollin and I were unsuccessful in getting <u>With All Odds Against Us</u> published.

Much of the material was later incorporated in a book titled <u>Hitler: Stalin's Stooge,</u> published in 2004.

APPENDIX 1

STATE OF THE ART IN THE CONTEXT OF
THE HISTORY OF ITS DEVELOPMENT
AS SEEN THROUGH THE EYES OF THE WRITER
AND AS RECORDED WHEN IT HAPPENED

CREDENTIALS
of
Rollin W. Gillespie

1 + 23 pages

CREDENTIALS
of
Rollin W. Gillespie

The following list of events in my career are listed, not as an autobiography, but as a history of space rocket development in the United States as experienced by one of the earliest participants. A minimum of strictly personal history is included only as context. It might have been useful to include the interactions of personalities as these influenced the decision process, but this is not the proper forum for that, and besides it would have made the document much too long. Suffice it to say that the manner in which important decisions were made, and not made, was in many cases very different from published versions. Just a few out of many examples include the $1^1/_2$ stage design of the Atlas rocket; the selection of Canaveral as the launch site; the decision to land men on the moon within the decade; the handshake with the Soviets in space; the choice of the Shuttle-space station complex; and the fatal launching of a Shuttle through the edge of a jet stream. A final comment: I enjoyed the "The Right Stuff" as much as anyone, but I looked in vain for some hint that the story of the space program is primarily a story of thousands of dedicated scientists, engineers, factory workers and others working anonymously for the most part, on a project bigger than themselves. It is that story which is reflected in the personal account which follows. I trust the account will be as fascinating as "The Right Stuff".

I was Born 7 April 1909 in my parents' home on their farm on Sac River, in the Missouri Ozarks, 12 miles northwest of Springfield, Missouri, and 24 airline miles from Marshfield, where Edwin Hubble was born and reared. I was told that the first word I ever said was "moon".

At the age of five years I hived a swarm of bees. My dad had gone to Springfield, and the bees swarmed, and clustered on the extremity of a limb high in an apple tree. Mother held a ladder, while I climbed it and sawed off the limb. I carried the bees down, and shook them in front of a hive, and they crawled inside. That was all there was to it. Thereafter I eagerly took full responsibility for caring for the entire apiary. In later years I conceived the notion that by artificially feeding a colony early in the season I could time the hatching of a large population of young bees to coincide with the blooming of white clover in June, and thus obtain a bountiful harvest. The experiment worked acording to script up to a point. The colony numbered several times as many individuals as a normal colony, all the right age to forage for nectar. But, instead of making honey, the bees developed swarming fever. The normal rhythm of instinctive behavior was so distorted for the main presentation in the speech. The main presentation showed and described our test results with fluorine-oxygen mixtures burned with gasolene. Needless to say Dave was surprized when he read the speech, but he had a sense of humor, and gave it just as I had prepared it. His was the first presentation on the agenda, and he told me that the discussion which followed lasted all day, allowing no time for other presentations. The outcome was as told in the preceding paragraph. Fluorine was from the beginning only an alternative for light weight engines and liquid hydrogen rocket fuel. Later, when these became assured, fluorine became obsolete.

I was the first to recognize the phenomenon of spin vibration in liquid propellant rocket combustion chambers. In February of 1952 a person who had participated in the testing of some 100 metric ton combustion chambers in the Soviet Union escaped to America, and when he was unable to find anyone in the Pentagon who appreciated what he had to say, he told it to private individuals. The Soviets had abandoned the program owing to persistent burnouts. They did not understand the cause of their problem, which I recognized at once—spin vibration. I immediately began the design of a larger combustion chamber, knowing that in time we would receive a request to do such a study. I guessed that the request would come from the Army in November of that year, delayed until immediately after the presidential election campaign during which spending cuts would be promised, and that the size would be specified in American tons, and rounded off to an even 300. In March I told top management that we would receive such a request in November. I was asked where I got such information, and said only that I generate it. I said that I planned to be the project manager, and if they had other ideas I would be the project engineer elsewhere, but that I would appreciate their views about the matter then rather than later. I was told that although they did not anticipate such a request there was no reason why I should not be the project engineer.

Three days after the November election I was awakened about 10:30 PM by a telephone call from one member of the management team who asked me if I knew there had been an all day session with representatives from the army, who had requested that Aerojet begin work on a 300 ton thrust chamber. Someone else had been assigned to be the project engineer. I had not been informed. Early next morning I was in the office of the president of the company when he arrived, to tell him that my resignation, tendered the previous March, was effective at 4:30 PM that day. (Later, at Rocketdyne, I was indeed for a time the project engineer on the large thrust chamber, based on my design, which became the prototype for the Saturn V rocket engines.)

If I may be forgiven for inserting an aside comment, President Kennedy was able to announce the NASA moon landing program only because Rocketdyne had already tested several large prototype engines. I know well what was going on in the rocket development companies across the nation at that time. I am firmly convinced that had I not pioneered the design of the large combustion chamber at Aerojet and then at Rocketdyne no one else would have done so on a timely basis, and it would have been politically impossible for the president to announce the moon landing program. Later such an announcement would have become impossible because of the war in Viet Nam.

While at Aerojet I organized Project ARC, with members from several organizations, industrial, governmental and academic, to promote space rockets. This led to my successful promotion of a contract with the Navy, through Al Satin in the Naval Research Laboratories, to design a satellite rocket. After I left Aerojet and before I went to Rocketdyne to work on the large light weight combustion chambers, I went to Washington, where I urged that the contract to design the rocket be left with Aerojet, and where I agreed that the Navy should ask Ed Heineman at Douglas to design the reentry vehicle. The three stages of the rocket were later assigned to different companies, and after much delay and many management problems placed the first American payload on earth parking orbit. After an on-off history, the reentry vehicle study ended at NACA Cleveland, where with the Air Force it was metamorphosed from a reentry vehicle to a supersonic research airplane—to be known as the X-15.

At Rocketdyne I was placed in charge of all of its 11 combustion chamber research programs. I also personally witnessed all of the first 151 test stand firings of the big Rocketdyne injectors.

I eliminated a persistent problem with wall burning in the Redstone combustion chamber by eliminating a curtain of fuel spray intended to cool the chamber wall, thereby reducing recirculation of combustion chamber gases, and thus largely eliminating scouring of the protective boundary layer from the wall. At the same time, the more uniform mixture ratio over the entire face of the injector resulted in an increase of 8% in the specific impulse of the propellants. Rocketdyne immediately informed the government of this result, and unilaterally raised the guaranteed level of performance by 8%.

Oxygen and JP-4 fuel was burned in the combustion chambers. Fuel rich mixtures were used, partly to reduce the flame temperature, but also in the belief that the deposits of soot protected the chamber wall from the heat.

After unsuccessful efforts to get the organization to increase the specific impulse by testing a more nearly stoichiometric mixture ratio, I arranged with one of the workers to transpose the propellant metering orifices by "mistake". By the time the "mistake" had been discovered, I had secured a mixture ratio survey in duplicate straddling the value which gives the highest specific impulse— and there had been no burned out thrust chamber.

I introduced a makeshift arrangement in which I placed "grasshopper" fittings in the ring channels behind the injector face to insure a more uniform flow and mixture ratio to all parts of the injector. Although these were intended only to demonstrate the need to improve the propellant distribution system they were retained as standard design.

I was responsible for the change in fuel specification from JP-4 to RP-1. The RP-1 fuel is essentially narrow cut kerosene with all the sulfur removed. JP-4 gave a predictable specific impulse in the main combustion chamber, but owing to its variable composition gave a highly unpredictable performance in the fuel rich gas generator for the pumps. Sulfur caused hydrogen embrittlement of the nickel tubes lining the combustion chamber, reducing their service life to about 50 seconds.

At this point I want to give credit to a lady whose name I do not remember, who described in her thesis for a Master's Degree at the University of British Columbia the mechanism whereby sulfur causes hydrogen embrittlement. I chanced to see her thesis. I do not believe she was ever informed of the important part her work had in the development of large rockets. Sulfur oxides in the combustion gases are reduced by excess fuel in the relatively cool boundary layer to produce hydrogen sulfide. The hydrogen sulfide rapidly decomposes and recomposes, temporarily releasing atomic hydrogen as an intermediate product. Atomic hydrogen is highly soluble in nickel, iron, etc, and penetrates to submicroscopic cavities in the crystal structure, where it combines with other atoms of hydrogen to form molecular hydrogen, which is insoluble. The hydrogen accumulates until enormous pressures are built up in the cavities. The process continues until every microscopic portion of the entire mass of the metal is loaded beyond the yield point, at which time it decomposes into black powder.

Apart from my work at Rocketdyne, and as an outside activity, I asked Al Wilson, then running the 50 inch Schmidt Camera sky survey at Mount Palomar Observatory, to consider leading a renewed Mars observation program, with the purpose of getting the astronomical community oriented toward the forthcoming use of rockets in astronomy. Al transferred to the

Lowell Observatory, where in a short time he became the director. I provided rocket planning, while Al organized the International Mars Committee. The committee sponsored a world wide program to photograph Mars during the favorable oppositions of 1954 and 1956.

Ernie Emery of Rocketdyne and I chartered a brand new Tripacer airplane and flew members of the Lowell staff, as well as Mr. Schneider, economic advisor to then Expresident Truman, and another man whose name I do not recall, the finance planner of the National Geographic Society, to various sites which might be considered for a new Space Astronomy Observatory. Meanwhile, Al used his influence to persuade four Texas oil millionaires to underwrite the cost of a new Space Astronomy Observatory. Since the Texas financiers insisted that the observatory be located in Texas, and since we considered Arizona to be a better location, the Governor of Arizona and the head of the Chamber of Commerce in Arizona were persuaded to sponsor the cession of several square miles of Arizona territory to Texas, with rights of ingress and egress. With plans for a new observatory already in being, the National Science Foundation seized the opportunity to take the funding of the project out of the hands of the Texas people. Thus was hatched what became the Kitt Peak Astronomical Observatory, and the 300 foot steerable dish radio astronomical telescope in West Virginia.

At JPL of CalTech I designed a 20000 pound thrust rocket test stand to burn chlorine trifluoride and hydrazine. It was built at Edwards Air Force Base. As far as I know, although it was the first fully automated test stand ever built, it was also the first rocket test stand in history to function flawlessly from the very first trial.

I supervised the theoretical calculation of the specific impulses of a comprehensive list of some 350 liquid propellant combinations. My complete list of oxidizers included two which had never been synthesized, but which as a result of my report were subsequently synthesized by the methods I suggested, and found to match my predictions. I was able to reduce the large number of possible combinations to a few best choices.

Just before, and mainly after, I left JPL late in 1957 I supervised the design by Henry Stephens, now deceased, of a 5000 pound splash plate injector. The splash plates formed annular pairs concentric with the axis of the combustion chamber. The feed system was designed to provide uniform flow and uniform mixture ratio over each tiny area of the entire injector face. Four units were built and tested on the test stand at Edwards Air Force Base in a series of tests extending over a one year interval. The injector was self cooled by the entering propellants, and in no case showed any visible scorching, although it was tested with chlorine trifluoride and hydrazine, one of the hottest burning propellant combinations known. There was no detectable vibration in any of the tests. The absence of vibration made it possible to obtain reliable measurements of pressure and thrust. Taking into account all minor corrections, such as nozzle throat coefficients etc, all the tests gave uniformly 101.4% of the theoretical specific impulse. The experimental results include substantially 100% of the theoretical performance plus additional performance resulting from the energy added by the velocity of the injected propellant streams.

The design of the injector can be directly scaled to any size. Moreover, it also lends itself to a cone shaped design which can reduce mass. Owing to the rapid mixing and burning, combustion is completed within a fraction of an inch of the injector face. Thus, the conical injector can do double duty as injector and combustion chamber, eliminating both the mass of the combustion chamber and the need to cool its wall.

I have been told that Boris Catorkin, who heads MASH, the Soviet factory which produces all the rockets made in the Soviet Union, is familiar with my name and the fact that I promoted the concentric splash plate injector. I dare say not one person in NASA Headquarters today is aware of the injector.

Don Bartz had been working on a theoretical equation to calculate the heat transfer from the combustion gases to the chamber wall. His long equation was filled with variables and arbitrary constants— and made very limited predictions. One day I had a flash of insight, and went to his office. He was gone, but his assistant, Calahan, was there, and I told him that the heat transfer depended entirely on the free energy present in a unit volume of the combustion gas, and on the rate at which the volume was renewed by the flow conditions. Bartz returned and Calahan relayed my thoughts to him. They quickly concluded that my model was correct, and Don did a good job educating others in a series of papers he presented at meetings. I am not aware that I was ever given credit, but I did not seek it.

In 1957, off the premises of JPL, I met with the president of Allied Chemical Company, the National Chief of Sales of their Nitrogen Division, and their West Coast Representative. I was in the key position in the JPL program to develop a chlorine trifluoride-hydrazine combustion chamber. The program was clasified SECRET. Allied had been allowed to believe there would be a market for chlorine trifluoride. I knew there would not be. Allied had already spent a million dollars starting the construction of a facility to manufacture chlorine trifluoride. I had been placed in an untenable ethical dilemma. I cannot justify either the decision I did make or the decision I did not make. What I did was contact their West Coast Representative, and suggest the company review very carefully the wisdom of spending any more money on the facility. I also told him that I planned to run some 5000 pound tests with nitrogen tetroxide and hydrazine, hopefully in the guise of developing chlorine trifluoride motors at JPL, but if not there, then at my own expense in an improvised test facility in the desert. I asked for some realistic price estimates for nitrogen tetroxide and for hydrazine in huge quantities. I reminded him that an Air Force edict some years before had terminated the nitrogen tetroxide-hydrazine test program at JPL, in which Allied was involved, and said that I intended to revive the program.

Allied thanked me profusely for having contacted them. They gave me a comprehensive and detailed report on every nitric acid plant in the United States, along with rail facilities and shipping costs and possibilities of conversion to nitrogen tetroxide— those of their own and those of their competitors. They had already done the paper work to get approval for shipping in tank cars. They gave me prices on hydrazine and also on unsymmetrical dimethyl hydrazine in quantity, radically less than the then current prices. In turn I was able to tell them that I had already tested at JPL some 5000 pound nitrogen tetroxide-hydrazine motors. They asked me what they could do to help. I replied that they would know better than I what to do.

In a few days JPL received an inquiry from the Secretary of the Army, Bruecker, whether JPL could show him a test of a nitrogen tetroxide-hydrazine motor. An appointment was set for Saturday. I stayed home, knowing I might not be able to keep a straight face. A few days later, both on the same morning, I received telephone calls from Rocketdyne and from Aerojet, wanting information on how to design big engines for an ICBM, using nitrogen tetroxide and hydrazine. I referred them to Don Lee, in JPL, who was the nation's foremost expert on hydrazine. No, they wanted to talk to me. It was thus that Aerojet reentered the big engine rocket business, with the Titan Rocket.

I wrote a letter to President Eisenhower proposing in detail the appointment of a Science Advisor to the President, and the creation of the Space Council, ARPA and NASA. I do not know whether the appointment of a science advisor was because of my letter, but an advisor was appointed, Dr. James Killian, President of Massachusetts Institute of Technology. As it happened I had the first appointment, for five minutes, with Killian when he reported for duty for the first time at his new office in the White House Office Building. Senator "Scoop" Jackson had the second appointment. My appointment was stretched to about two hours, and Senator Jackson was still waiting when I finished.

Killian wanted to know why I had recommended CalTech and not MIT in my letter to Eisenhower regarding the creation of a space agency. I told him that it was because CalTech had a number of experienced rocket scientists, and that as far as I was aware MIT had none. He did not pursue the matter further. I showed him a strip photo copied from Sputnik II transmissions and converted into a photograph by a young man named Brown at JPL of Cal Tech. I explained that I had been careful not to involve Brown in my decision to come to Washington, and that no one in JPL knew I was there. The reason was that I believed that to transmit my message through the normal channels would almost certainly result in the Soviets knowing we had deciphered the Sputnik code, probably before the message would reach Washington.

The strip photograph covered a great circle path beginning at the sunrise in the western Pacific and ending in the evening haze over the Atlantic Ocean. The sunrise was marked by a diagonal boundary across the strip, owing to the angle at which the path intersected the edge of the sunlit hemisphere. Hawaii was shown, and northern Canada. One of the Pine Tree stations was shown, west of Churchill. I pointed out that neither we nor the Soviets knew within 20 miles the relative positions of Moscow and New York on the face of the earth. This information would be vital for aiming ICBM's. I also pointed out that our Dew Line and Pine Tree stations would serve as beacons to guide Soviet missiles to their intended targets, using offset aiming. As an aside I told Killian that our 1500 mile rockets in Turkey would be useless in a war with the Soviets for the reason that Turkey, being vulnerable to easy retaliation by the Soviets, could not allow us to launch them from her territory. At this point Killian sent for a man whose name I do not recall, the chief of technology evaluations in the CIA.

The CIA man told us that what I showed them would explain why the Soviets had had 13 submarines on the surface of the ocean, 6 on one side and 7 on the other of Canada, during that particular Sputnik crossing over Canada. I emphasized the importance of keeping the Soviets in the dark about our decipherment, and suggested a set of instructions to be given our armed forces world wide regarding the collection of all tape recordings, and making better ones next time, which I believed would be within two or three months. I said that next time we should have aircraft flying ready to jam the reception of radio signals by Soviet submarines. He asked me to write down a set of instructions in a form suitable for transmission. Then he left, and returned shortly with the White House red telephone. He read my instructions, then handed me the telephone and asked me to read them myself. The scrambled message was sent simultaneously to every American military base on the entire earth, in my own voice.

During the crossings of North America by Sputnik III our fighter planes were ready, and buzzed the Soviet submarines. The Soviets complained in the United Nations, and Adlai Stephenson, our Ambasador to the United Nations replied that, "yes, we did, and we will do it again." The Soviets never raised the question again. Adlai had unintentionally told them that we had deciphered the Sputnik code, and that was all they needed to know.

I should insert a personal note. My unauthorized actions leaked out, and triggered a series of responses by JPL management and lower echelons in CIA. Froelich, assistant to the director of JPL, Dr. Pickering, made a special trip to Washington, where he fired me on the steps of the White House Office Building. He acted properly within the limited information at his disposal. On my return flight to Los Angeles the pilot came back to my seat to check my identity, with one result that we subsequently carried on a correspondence about ball lightning. I was surprized not to be apprehended when I landed in Los Angeles. Dr. Pickering arranged for me to be employed in the company of my choice, which was the Missiles and Space Division of Lockheed at Sunnyvale. I was reemployed there with a substantial increase in salary. Later, at Drury College, I was named Drury Alumnus of the Year, at the request of certain elected officials in Washington. The science editors of a half dozen newspapers such as Time Magazine and the New York Times sat incognito in the audience. To this day Drury does not know what I did to merit the honor.

Eisenhower sent my letter to the Joint Chiefs of Staff in the Pentagon, and they forwarded it to Senator "Stu" Symington, who was the first Chairman of the newly formed Senate Space Committee. I was invited by Symington to his home, where I spent a day and much of the night briefing him on the status of rocketry in America and in the Soviet Union. As we parted he told me that my proposal was the first recommendation that made sense, and that it would be written into law. This was done, with a few minor additions.

At the Lockheed Missiles and Space Division my supervisor was Wolfgang Noegerath. He supervised personnel while I supervised the design of a liquid hydrogen-liquid oxygen rocket by 100 people. Lockheed did not win the contract to build the rocket, but the design was the basis for the hydrogen rockets which were built by other companies.

After five months of intensive work on my own time evenings and weekends I came up with the insight which enabled my colleagues John Breakwell and Stan Ross, also at Lockheed, to perfect the equation by which one could select a trajectory which would carry a spacecraft from one moving planet to another moving planet. I requested permission from the management to give copies of our computer program to anyone who might make good use of it, and within three days had permission from the Chairman of the Board himself. Every interplanetary flight ever made has used our equation.

We gave our paper at the 14th Annual Meeting of the American Rocket Society in November, 1959, in Washington, D.C. Blagonrovov, Chief of the Soviet Rocket Program, and his boss, Sedov, President of the Soviet Academy of Sciences came for the meeting, and sought us out at the authors' breakfast. They had purchased the entire stack of preprints, and asked us to autograph some of them. It took us more than a year to get our paper published in America, but they published it in Russia without our permission, which we would have given if asked, within three months. Immediately afterward they launched the first interplanetary rocket, intended to go to Venus. Next day they announced that they had lost contact with it. Unfortunately, our machine calculations had an error— a plus where there should have been a minus— and we had not detected the error at the time we gave our paper. We did detect it immediately afterward, and would have notified the Soviets had we known they were going to publish it. I surmise they launched the Venus rocket on the wrong trajectory. I can only hope they did not believe we deliberately included the error.

Wehrner von Braun had persuaded President Kennedy to announce the start of the "Nova" rocket program. The announcement was scheduled to be made publicly before Congress the middle of February 1962. The Lockheed Washington Office notified us of the decision the same day it was made, Friday, 19 January, twelve days before the end of January, and I heard about it about the middle of the afternoon. I had just invented and completed the first "Pork Chop" diagram of interplanetary trip opportunities, and had started to design a hypothetical flight, with appropriate maneuvers and discards of mass. I immediately rolled up my papers and drove home, and worked without sleep from Friday afternoon until Sunday afternoon. By then I had calculated a sample round trip vehicle for each of Mars and Venus. The "Nova" rocket would be a mistake. Early Monday morning I handed my supervisor a sealed letter containing my resignation, to be opened only if Lockheed should choose not to go with me. I proposed that I would go to Washington, with or without Lockheed support, to kill the president's announcement before it would be made. I pointed out that the time was short. Three days afterward top management at Burbank sent word that Lockheed would go with Gillespie.

I paid a courtesy visit to Huntsville, together with my supervisory staff. Wehrner von Braun was out of town, but Hermann Koelle brought in the entire engineering staff to hear my presentation. That evening, after we were gone, when Wehrner returned he was given a briefing by Koelle, and issued instructions that the entire engineering staff stop whatever else it was doing and check my calculations. A week later Harry Ruppe took their finding to Washington, and Kennedy's announcement was cancelled.

I was widely credited as being the first to see how to set up the equation by which to preselect an interplanetary transfer trajectory. Some 114 competent mathematicians had in the past tried and failed, and at the time I made my contribution there were six government contracts, all of which failed. Lockheed did not have a contract. However, I wish here to set the record straight. It was only several years later, when I was in Washington, that I invited ---- Lascody, then at Douglas Aircraft, to visit over night in our home in McLean, Virginia. Then for the first time I learned that had also solved the problem, slightly earlier than I, at Douglas. Not only so, but he too had independently invented the "Pork Chop" diagram. Unfortunately, his company's policies regarding proprietary rights had prevented both him and Douglas from exploiting his discovery, and at the same time denied him the credit he should have had.

Jim Stephens, of JPL, worked closely with me in planning a comprehensive space transportation system. All my official activities were in fact parts of this unofficial activity. We visited South Point, Hawaii, which I believe is by far the best location in the entire world for an interplanetary spaceport.

While we were in Hawaii we carried a spectrograph to the site on Mauna Kea then under consideration for a proposed new astronomical observatory, which was subsequently built. This was the instrument which had been generating data on the high slopes of Mauna Loa, and which continued to generate data on Mauna Kea— data which revealed the buildup of carbon dioxide in the earth's atmosphere. The road up the mountain had not yet been extended as far as the proposed site, and we had to carry the spectrograph on foot for the final part of the journey.

We visited Jim's Uncle Ernie Henderson, head of the Sheraton Hotel Chain. Ernie told me that he could cash out his hotel holdings for $39 million, and that he would do so to support our proposal if we could assure him his contribution would not lose its identity by being smothered by federal money. Later at LMSD I received a telephone call from Bob Gross, Chairman of the Lockheed Board of Directors in Burbank. Ernie was in Bob's office discussing a plan to build individual housing units for my proposed base at South Point. Was it agreeable with me for them to continue the discussion? I said I did not believe my permission was necessary, but that it was certainly agreeable with me. They actually entered into a joint arrangement to build a motel complex in California as a trial venture between the two companies, to gain experience for the proposed venture in Hawaii. One week later Bob discovered that he had cancer of the pancreas, and called off the venture in order to devote all his remaining few weeks of life to reorganizing the various Lockheed plants for greater local autonomy.

While at LMSD I attended a symposium on rockets sponsored by the Navy in San Francisco. The president of Allied Chemical Company spotted me in the lobby, and invited me to join him and the president of United Aircraft, which I did. He again thanked me for alerting his company not to spend a big sum to build a chlorine trifluoride plant. He asked me how I was progressing in my plan to design a comprehensive space transportation system. The three of us spent the day together. At the end I was asked to carry to Lockheed a proposal to activate my plan, in which United would enter a joint venture in which it would manufacture rocket engines, and Lockheed would manufacture the remaining structures and operate the facilities. Allied asked me to carry a separate proposal, in which it would at its own expense build and operate the liquid hydrogen, liquid nitrogen and liquid oxygen plant at South Point. Both men understood fully that I was only a promoter, and not speaking for the Management of Lockheed. I took the proposals to my management at LMSD, and pointed out, and they agreed, that the proposals required a reply from Top Management at Burbank. One result was the creation of the space division within the Lockheed Missiles and Space Division. As far as I ever knew, that was about all that came out of the proposals.

Late in 1962 I was to give a paper in Los Angeles describing my proposed single-stage-to-orbit rocket. Sid Brown, my boss third removed up the line, was to preside over the session, in which I was scheduled to give the first presentation. On the last day before, Von Braun telephoned Sid to say that he would prefer that the paper not be given. What could Sid do, other than what he did do, namely say that my paper was not yet ready? My trip to Los Angeles was cancelled.

I decided on a trip to Los Angeles on my own. Next morning, as Sid was making a few opening remarks, and just as he explained that unfortunately I was not ready to present my paper, I strode down the isle on one side of the auditorium, across in front of the audience of some 300, and back out up the isle on the other side. I then went back to the airport.

In a few days I received a telephone call from the Space Council, asking me, "What was that all about?" I was asked to come to Washington at my convenience. When I did so I was told that the President had told them to go out and bring in all those Gillespies to NASA headquarters. Of course Kennedy did not know me personally, and only used my name in a generic sense. This is how I happened to join the Civil Service in NASA headquarters.

In 1969 I was preparing a proposal for a comprehensive space transportation program. I was ordered in writing to destroy all copies of the proposal, and confine my work to the Shuttle. I could not in good conscience continue to accept my salary at the highest level in the Civil Service and remain silent and work on the shuttle, which I regarded as a big mistake. Instead, later that same day I made 100 copies of the incompleted proposal, distributed 50 copies to top management in NASA headquarters, and mailed the rest to individuals all over the country. I then waited to be fired, and when that did not happen, I retired.

Since my retirement in 1969 I have actively pursued a number of research projects, some growing out of space research, and some not.

1. I show how the sun and the planets exchange angular momentum. They now oscillate narrowly around an equilibrium in which the angular rate of rotation of the sun at its equator must be and is almost exactly twice the sum of the angular rates of revolution of all the planets.

2. I show that each of the planets, one after the other, formed just above the Roche radius of the sun. Uranus, Saturn and Jupiter each now rotates at a rate it inherited from the time it was just above the Roche radius, when its period of rotation was the same as its period of revolution, namely 10 hours, set by the gravitational attraction of the sun on a tidal bulge on the planet. The theory also neatly accounts for the rotation rates of Neptune and the inner planets. A transfer of angular momentum slowed the rotation of the sun and expanded the orbits of the planets in accordance with harmonic principles. Mars once had a sister planet which escaped to the outer reaches of the solar system, wreaking havoc as it went.

It was I who first recognized the phenomenon of spin vibration in liquid propellant rocket motors, and its cause and cure. The story of rocket engine development is a story of burned out combustion chambers. And it would be my estimate that spin vibration destroyed more high-performance combustion chambers than all other causes combined. What happens in spin vibration is that a sound wave travels around and around inside the combustion chamber, with a frequency corresponding to a wave length of approximately 57 percent of the inside circumference of the chamber. Like any vibration, it can be eliminated by damping, detuning and decoupling. In view of the resistance to the very concept of spin vibration on the part of others for a time extending over months and years, it seems possible that we might have gone on for years without having a large, efficient and dependable rocket engine, had it not been for my presence on the job.

I was the first to successfully burn liquid fluorine in a rocket
motor. And it was I who discovered that the density of liquid fluorine
was almost 40 percent greater than the literature value. Within days
after my first test, I received a delegation of Air Force officials who
had been awaiting either a high energy propellant or a light weight
engine to justify a program to develop the intercontinental rocket
mentioned on page 10 of Chapter 11. Because my chief test operator
had come down with influenza, a "B-nut" was not tightened in the
fluorine feed line, and we had a fire. No one panicked, and every man
coolly carried out his duties according to the plan for such an emergency. Within an hour I was able to announce to our visitors that we
would be ready for a repeat operation the following morning. They
informed me that the fact that we had been able to control the fire
had made a much greater impression on them than a successful test would
have done, and that they knew of no test stand fire even with ordinary
propellant combinations which had been repaired within less than a week.
On the spot they initiated the program which produced the Atlas Intercontinental Ballistic Rocket. Fortunately the light weight engine
became available in time to make it unnecessary to use the high-energy
fluorine propellant combination.

THEORETICAL PROPELLANT CALCULATIONS

Later I calculated the theoretical performances of several hundred
propellant combinations. These included two oxidizers which, as far as
I could ascertain, had never been mentioned in the literature, and had
never been made. Both were subsequently synthesized, and both had
properties close to my predictions. But the important result of my
work was the revival of the use of dinitrogen tetroxide and hydrazine.
In 1951 someone in the Air Force had issued an edict terminating all
research with that propellant combination under Air Force contracts.
The orders had been definite— anyone who had any qualifying notions
could leave. Several did. But in 1958 the Allied Chemical Company
had begun construction of an expensive plant to manufacture
chlorine trifluoride, at their own expense, in the misinformed belief

that there would be a substantial market for the product in a secret
project. I was placed in an impossible position of abiding by the
security restrictions under which I had accepted employment and of
warning the company that they were being misled behind a smoke screen of
military secrecy. I made a choice. I contacted the company representative and suggested his company review carefully their own judgement
about the market for the oxidizer. I also reminded him that his
company had been the chief commercial participant in the dinitrogen
tetroxide and hydrazine program in 1951, and I asked him to provide
me cost estimates for large quantities of the oxide and of hydrazine.
I told him I would make demonstration tests of the propellant combination in 5000-pound thrust chambers before the end of the summer,
either in the laboratory where I worked or in a facility I would
construct out in the desert at my own expense.

One month later I was invited out to lunch with the field
representative, together with the chief of the sales division of
Allied Chemical Company and the president of their Nitrogen Products
Division. They thanked me profusely for my suggestion, and spread on
the table a detailed map of all nitric acid plants in the United
States, theirs and their competitors', showing the cost of manufacture
and delivery from the cheapest source to any point in the country of
dinitrogen tetroxide. Not only that, but they also provided similar
data on hydrazine and unsymmetrical dimethyl hydrazine, and they had
already initiated steps to gain Interstate Commerce Commission
approval for shipping these products in railroad tank cars. For my
part I was able to tell them that I had already begun a series of
tests in 5000-pound combustion chambers of the propellant combination.
They asked me what they could do to help matters along, and I told
them that they should use their influence at the highest level to
see that a top representative of the military establishment should
ask to see the tests. Within a few days Secretary of the Army Brueker
asked to see them, and I stayed home that day to avoid any suggestion
I might be involved in the maneuver. Less than two weeks later both
Rocketdyne and Aerojet were instructed by their Air Force contracting
agency to contact me personally for information on setting up a program
to use the "new" propellant combination in large motors as a potential

replacement for the Atlas engine, which used oxygen and kerosene. The
rest of the story is well known history— Aerojet got back into the big
rocket engine business with the dinitrogen tetroxide-unsymmetrical
dimethyl hydrazine propellant combination.

I leave it to the reader to determine for himself whether I did
the right thing. I should add that I pulled off similar stunts throughout my rocket career; that in no single case did I ever take advantage
of my "inside" information to benefit myself personally; that at the
time and now in retrospect I believe the rocket program would have
suffered great loss, and in some cases death had I not taken the actions
I took; and that then and now in retrospect I do not believe I could
have accomplished what I did by following the accepted course of resign-
ing and working from outside. One final comment— to do what I did one
must be right and one must know one is right. There is no room for
error.

LARGE ENGINE PROTOTYPE

In February 1952 the Russians tested a 100-metric ton thrust
chamber. It failed because of spin vibration— a phenomenon they had
not recognized, and had never heard of. In early March one of their
workmen managed to escape from Russia and come to the United States,
where he encountered non-comprehension among the defense department
representatives with whom he talked. He met with some private citizens
and told his story.

I recognized that the implication of his story would permeate the
Pentagon after a few months, but that by then the presidential campaign
would be in progress, and that campaign rhetoric about economy would
delay action until after the election. We would then be asked to
develop a large thrust chamber. The size would have to exceed the 100
metric tons of the Russian thrust chamber, and it would be in pounds.
Moreover, lacking any other guide to its proposed size it would be a
rounded-off figure. Since the first rounded-off size beyond 100 metric
tons (220,000 pounds) is 300,000 pounds, I knew what the size would be,
300,000 pounds.

I went to the top management of the company where I worked at the
time (Aerojet) and stated that we would receive a request from the
military to design a 300,000-pound thrust chamber about one or two
weeks after the first of November of that year, and that it was my
intention to have the design already completed before that time, and
that I planned to be the project engineer. If Aerojet had other
plans, I said, then I wanted to know immediately so that I could phase
out the work I was doing there and arrange to be working elsewhere.
I was told that Aerojet knew of no such upcoming project, and was
asked where I got my information. My answer was that I generate such
information! "Well, we don't expect anything like that to happen, but
if it does we see no reason you cannot be the project engineer." Came
the third day after the election in November, a delegation of army
people came to Aerojet and requested a bid on a 300,000 pound thrust
chamber study. I learned about it that night after I had gone to bed
and was asleep. And I learned that another person had been selected
to be the project engineer! Needless to say I left Aerojet very
promptly, and continued my unofficial design work at Rocketdyne.
After a couple of years my work there resulted in a prototype engine
contract calling for a 600,000-pounds thrust chamber. For a time I
was the project engineer— just long enough to keep the record straight,
for I had other more pressing projects by that time. It is my
opinion that had I not promoted the big engine program at the time I
did, the United States would not have had the technology on which to
base the political decision to send men to the moon in the 1960's,
and that had that political decision not been made when it was made
it would have been too late to make it at all.

FORMATION OF NASA AND ARPA

After the Russians placed the first "Sputnik" in orbit around the
earth I wrote a letter to President Eisenhower recommending that all
rocket development be taken out of the hands of the military organization and placed in a new agency to be created for the purpose. Then,
any rocket development which would not contribute to a space effort
should be taken from the new agency and placed in still another new
agency to be created for the purpose within the military establishemnt.

Not long afterward Senator Stu Symington spent an entire day and part
of an evening with me in his home discussing my proposal. He told me
the letter had been forwarded to the Joint Chiefs of Staff for them
to take appropriate action. In the end he told me that it was the best
plan, and indeed the only plan which anyone had proposed which made
sense, and that the Congress would act favorably on it. The plan
provided for the transfer of the Jet Propulsion Laboratory of Cal Tech
and of a part of Redstone Arsenal in Alabama to the new agency. On
a later occasion Dr. James Killian, the president's science advisor,
asked me why I had not included MIT, where he had been the head man
before coming to Washington. I told him why, namely that JPL had a
reservoir of experienced rocket people, and MIT did not have. He
seemed satisfied. The new agencies were created very nearly along the
lines I had recommended— NASA and ARPA.

KEPLER'S PROBLEM

By the time I arrived in Lockheed in 1958 a great many changes had
taken place in the national rocket effort and in my personal life. I
was able to provide the technical guidance for a 100-man team to design
a hydrogen-oxygen rocket. The study provided the basis for a government
decision to abandon fluorine propellant combinations in favor of hydrogen and oxygen as the chosen high energy propellant combination. But
the contract to develop the engine was placed elsewhere, and I began a
new phase in my rocket career. I undertook to solve what had long been
known to mathematicians as Kepler's problem. Given the elements of an
orbit, Kepler's equations will predict the future positions of a particle in a gravitational field, say of a rocket around the sun. However,
what Kepler's equations do not do is specify the elements of an orbit
which will take a rocket from here and now to there and then, say from
the earth at a given moment and to Mars at a later given moment. I
devised the concept of the solution, and with Drs. John Breakwell and
Stanley Ross (to provide the mathematics which I lacked) developed the
practical solution of the problem. Every interplanetary flight ever
made, whether by the Americans or the Russians, has depended on the
procedure which we developed.

MANNED PLANETARY TRIP PLANNING

On a friday afternoon about ten days before the end of January 1962 the word came to us in Lockheed that President Kennedy planned an announcement about the 15th of February that the government would go ahead with a huge rocket (vaguely defined and known as "Nova"). Wehrner von Braun was sponsoring the rocket, and had convinced the president that it was the proper design and size to do whatever needed to be done in space. By one of those coincidences which make history I had just completed that very day a chart showing the available trajectories for a Venus trip, and I had the computer data to prepare such a chart for Mars. This Venus chart was the first such chart in history, and without it no one knew, or could even guess the propulsion requirements for an interplanetary trip.

When I heard the news I locked my desk and took my data and charts home, and worked almost around the clock until after midnight on Sunday night. By that time I had calculated the propulsion requirements for a round trip journey to each of the two planets, Venus and Mars. My findings revealed that the "Nova" was very inappropriate for the job it was expected to perform. On Monday morning I handed my supervisor a sealed envelop containing my letter of resignation, effective the date of opening. I told him what was in the envelop, and asked him not to open the envelop until he had discussed the matter with his superiors. We agreed that the decision would have to be made at the highest level in the company. The decision: I was going to Washington to kill that program before it would be announced; either I would go alone without Lockheed, or with Lockheed. Within three days the decision came down from the Chairman of the Board—Lockheed management would go with Gillespie! This, mind you, in spite of the fact that Lockheed already had over one hundred people working on the "Nova" at company expense.

We went first to Huntsville, where the entire propulsion group listened and understood what we told them. They were very excited to have for the first time data by which to put significant numbers into their calculations. We went on to Washington, where we gave several presentations to small groups who did not fully understand what we told them. Meanwhile, von Braun gave orders for everyone in his organization to drop everything else and check my figures. Within the week they had the answer— Gillespie was right, but the actual weight requirements were even worse than I had allowed. Von Braun sent Harry Ruppe to Washington with the news, and the president cancelled his planned announcement.

FIVE YEARS IN NASA

It was a year later that I received a telephone call from the Space Council inviting me to Washington, where I was told that the president, although he did not know me even remotely, had declared that he wanted to bring the "Gillespies" into the government. He had been shocked more than once to find a unanimous approval within the establishment of a program in which some outsider could point out some fatal flaw.

In NASA I served as a very useful, although many times unwelcome conscience. In 1969 I resigned because I found myself in a minority of one in opposition to the space shuttle and orbiting space laboratory program. I liked my job, and the work. I had a Civil Service Grade 16-6 salary. I was only 60 years old, and healthy. But I had been ordered not to circulate or discuss the study I had prepared for a national space program. NASA had fallen into the familiar trap of trying to justify a program by suppressing any discussion of alternatives. This was something "up with which I could not put". I had circulated a half dozen copies of my proposal, "A TOTAL UNIFIED PLAN FOR SPACE RESEARCH AND SOLAR SYSTEM EXPLORATION THROUGHOUT THE NEXT 35 YEARS", 15 February 1969. When I was ordered to call in those copies I immediately went personally to the Xerox machine and made 100 copies, and personally laid a copy on the desk of each person in the line of management above me. Then I distributed the remainder to individuals all over the United States, in NASA centers and in companies. I then waited to be fired, and when that did not happen I resigned.

The proposal in abbreviated form will be presented in the final section of this chapter.

A NITROGEN TETROXIDE HYDRAZINE ICBM 1959

By
Rollin W. Gillespie
22 April 1993

During the interval between November and April of 1958-1959, after I left JPL and before I reported for duty in Lockheed, Henry Stephens and his son Jim, and I together designed an intercontinental ballistic missile which we called a "ready rocket". I have lost my copy of the original papers, but Jim has a copy which he will insert here in this document.

Denton Smith, boyhood neighbor of myself, of Springfield, Missouri, and now deceased, responded immediately to my telephoned request for financial help. He owned and managed a successful manufacturing operation, but told me he regarded the opportunity to take part in so important a technological project as a high light in his life. He had no expectation of a financial return on his investment, which came to a total of around $ 6000.

Denton and I together took the proposed design to Senator Stu Symington, who chaired the newly formed Senate Space Committee. Stu was cordial, and understood our proposal. He told us that he could not act on the proposition without first clearing it with his close friend Dutch Kindleberger, Founder and Chairman of the Board of North American Aviation. He explained that when he went to Los Angeles he stayed in Dutch's home, and when Dutch came to Washington he stayed in Stu's home. Dutch had favored him by building the Atlas engine plant in Missouri. I immediately understood that we had gone to the end of the road, and handed Stu a spare copy of the proposal and told him to send it to Dutch. I had the satisfaction of seeing 23 innovations in the design incorporated into the design of the Saturn V rocket.

It was during this interval that Von Braun came to Rocketdyne on a Friday, and announced his plan to build the Saturn I rocket. Jim was in the meeting. Von Braun said he would return on Monday morning to discuss details. Jim went home and designed the Saturn I from scratch, based on the cluster tank design of our rocket. Came Monday morning, and he presented the complete drawings for the Saturn I, saying to Von Braun, "Is this what you are looking for?" The design was accepted, and built. As far as I know not a single bolt or fitting was altered.

THE JPL INJECTOR
By
Rollin W. Gillespie
14 April 1993

I have mentioned the JPL injector in different parts of this paper. I had promoted a concept I called the tube bundle manifold propellant feed system at Rocketdyne, and then at JPL. At JPL I asked one of the draftsmen to attempt a design embodying the concept. Before I had seen his first effort, Jack Froelich, Deputy to the General Manager, saw it, and promptly sent orders to my boss to remove me from all injector design activities, then and in the future. I subsequently arranged for JPL to hire Henry Stephens. He and I discussed the concept several times, both before and after I left JPL. He designed a 5000-lb injector.

Four units were built, and tested over a period of a year at Edwards Air Force Base on the 20000-lb test stand whose construction I had supervised for testing chlorine trifluoride and hydrazine propellants. This injector design is the one which consistently in all four units gave a specific impulse of 101.4% efficiency calculated in the usual manner, and taking into account the throat coefficient of the nozzle (actually 100% theoretical specific impulse plus 1.4% attributable to the energy of motion of the injected propellant streams). The measurement was very reliable owing to the total lack of vibration. Nor was there the slightest scorching of the copper faced injector, in spite of the fact that the propellants were chlorine trifluoride and hydrazine, one of the hottest burning propellant combinations.

The propellants impinged on concentric pairs of splash plates, alternately fuel and oxidizer, from orifices arranged in concentric circles around the center line of the injector. The splash plates were circular sections cut from thin copper cones. Thus the propellant streams were spread into thin sheets before coming together. Mixing and burning were both completed within a fraction of an inch from the edges of the splash plates.

Although the propellants are extremely hypergolic, the same result would be expected from other combinations, inasmuch as the open spacs between the pairs of concentric ring splash plates are filled with hot combustion products, causing them to act as flame holders.

One important fealture of the design is that it is scalable to any size. Another is that it can be modified from a flat face to a hollow cone face, thus reducing the mass of the injector, but more importantly eliminating entirely the need for a cylindrical combustion chamber. The nozzle would be attached directly to the cone. The propellant density would be made uniform across the flat cross section of the cone, thus insuring that each ring of burned gas would flow parallel to the axis of the motor toward the nozzle, and act as an igniter to the next outer (and adjacent) ring of propellant spray.

The contraction ratio of the nozzle can be made almost equal to 1.0, probably slightly more to anchor the sonic cross section of the gas, and to reduce the required pump outlet pressure. Rocketdyne tested throatless motors in which oxygen and JP-1 were injected from extremely fine orifices, and burned within a fraction of an inch of the injector face. They performed according to theory. One possible shortcoming in the Rocketdyne injector is that the slightest speck of dirt can clog an orifice.

A prominent feature of the design is that it does not depend on macroturbulence for mixing the propellants. It is precisely this feature which makes possible the high efficiency of the JPL injector. Macroturbulence automatically requires that some portions of the propellant recirculate in the combustion space, thus requiring a greater than average dwell time in the chamber at the expense of dwell time for other portions of the propellant. The inevitable result is that some of the propellant emerges from the nozzle before being mixed and burned. No reasonable amount of characteristic length (L*) of the combustion chamber can avoid this problem. Only microturbulence can do it. And imicroturbulence in the JPL design avoids the problem by eliminating altogether the need for a combustion chamber.

Another feature is the uniform distribution of propellant flow and mixture ratio over the cross section of the injector. This is accomplished not only by the injector orifice pattern, but by the design of the propellant feed lines. Henry Stephens showed that more than two outlets from a propellant feed line will have unequal flow rates, but that two outlets can have equal flow rates. This is demonstrated in blood vessels, which divide into two, but never more. He devised a series of plates, with orifices, which when stacked divided the propellant flow into pairs, and then subdivided it into sub-pairs, etc.

Still another feature was the incorporation of a high pressure drop between the pressurized feed tanks and the injector, thus minimizing the pulsations in flow which result from cavitation at the flow metering orifices. Jerry Elverum at JPL demonstrated the effect of cavitation by flowing water through the metering orifices. Standing in the test bay the noise sounded like gravel being carried through the feed lines.

Henry Stephens and his son Jim (now at JPL), together with myself, designed on paper a pump fed rocket in which the pumps were mounted with their axes on the longitudinal axis of the combustion chamber. The propellant tanks opened directly into the pump inlets. The diffusion vanes around the impeller rim were attached to a slip ring in the manner of a camera diaphragm shutter so that the pump outlet pressure at varying flow rate could be controlled to facilitate throttling of the rocket motor. (I have been told that Aerojet has done some tsting of such a pump design.)

In addition instead of a single volute which collects all the flow into one chamber and redistributes it to the injector orifices, the particular pump design had 31 outlets, each feeding its assigned portion of the injector face. This feature reduces the volume of the feed lines, facilitating smooth start up and shut down, and also providing ballanced loads on the pump impeller shafts. But the main purpose of the design was to retain the already uniformly divided propellant flow to avoid multiple dividing and redividing of a single flow. In this way the volume of the feed lines is reduced, and water hammer problems minimized.

The performance of the JPL injector demonstrates that the state of the art already in 1959 permitted of highly efficient and predictable rocket engine designs. The problem in 1993 is not whether this represents the state of the art, but whether practitioners of the art have yet caught up with 1959.

APPENDIX 11

DESIGN OF CHEMICAL ROCKETS   LOCKHEED   1962

By
Rollin W. Gillespie
2 May 1993

1+55 pages

DESIGN OF A CHEMICAL ROCKET FOR
MANNED INTERPLANETARY EXPEDITIONS

by

Rollin W. Gillespie

ABSTRACT

This paper presents a concept of a large chemical rocket. With a single-stage, it carries 666 metric tons of cargo to earth-parking orbit for use in manned interplanetary exploration. An annual market for a dozen rockets is indicated. Oxygen-hydrogen and oxygen-propane are given special attention. The propane rocket has a launch mass of 12,000 metric tons, a diameter of 20 meters, and a height of 100 meters. Pressure-stabilized tanks and a plug-nozzle engine are used. Most of the cargo is propellant, which is carried as excess in the tanks of the main stage. 5.5 percent of the launch mass is useful cargo on parking orbit. Reliability is sought by use of theory already experimentally verified, and by reduction in the need for men at the launch site. The rocket is expected to cost less than any other rocket system, and to make possible the earliest fully operational date possible by any means.

Section 1

INTRODUCTION

Rocketry is now at a point of transition between learning how to design, facilitate, and operate rockets, and using rockets as tools in space exploration. Recent works by the author and his colleagues (Refs. 1 to 7) have provided orbit mechanics theory and data by which it is now possible to specify in detail the propulsion maneuvers for entire round-trip flyby and landing expeditions to Mars and Venus at every opportunity which presents itself between 1960 and 1999. This paper presents the concept that a large, single-stage rocket can best meet the requirements of a manned, interplanetary rocket program. Such a rocket can be designed from existing theory, already experimentally verified. For this reason the cost can be kept reasonable, the rocket can be made available early, and its reliability should be enhanced.

The aim of this paper is to present, and not to prove, this concept. Therefore, supporting material has largely been omitted, and the author hopes that the many statements which are made without elaboration will be neither accepted nor rejected, but held in suspended judgement until the broad outline of the concept is apparent.

Section 4

ROCKET CONFIGURATION

Figure 2 compares a single-stage oxygen-propane rocket with the SATURN C-5 and a postulated 12,000,000-pound-thrust version of NOVA. The propane rocket has about 3.4 times the mass of the NOVA, and places 3.7 times the mass of cargo on earth parking orbit.

Figure 3 is a schematic arrangement of the rocket in both the propane and hydrogen modifications. The engine is an improvement on the plug-nozzle engine proposed by Kurt Berman (Ref. 8), and extensively developed by General Electric Company and others. The plug-nozzle cone is gas filled, and pressure stabilized. In the apex of the cone is a small motor which is ignited at the moment of launching, and which continues to act as a vernier motor after the main engine is stopped on orbit.

The propellants are carried in the cylindrical section, made up of two pressure-stabilized tanks in tandem. The oxygen tank is aft of the fuel tank, since this results in the least structural mass, especially in the hydrogen rocket. In the case of the propane rocket, but not the hydrogen rocket, it would be feasible to use concentric tanks, with the denser oxygen in the center. However, the structure would at the same time be more massive and less rugged. One attractive modification would be a concentric oxygen tank within the lower portion only of a full-length propane tank. The arrangement shown is therefore to be taken as typical, and not necessarily as the only one.

The pressure-stabilized nose cone has room for many customized interplanetary packages. Although the cylindrical section of the rocket could be shortened by letting the fuel tank extend into the cone, it was thought best to distribute the cargo-mass over as large an area as possible, to reduce the tank pressure required to support the load.

No doubt the discarded mass can be reduced by improvements in design and acceleration schedule, by selection of different materials, and by reduction in the safety factor. However, the issue is not a critical one. Figure 11 shows the sensitivity of both rockets to variations in discarded mass, and variations in engine specific impulse. At the design point specifications, the launch mass of the hydrogen rocket is only 53 percent that of the propane rocket, but the height is greater. It is seen that the point is on the flat part of the hydrogen curve, but that it is near the steep portion of the propane curve. The propane rocket would require some oversizing to allow for uncertainties in discard-mass and in specific impulse. In spite of this unfavorable comparison with the hydrogen rocket, the propane rocket is still operating within its satisfactory speed range.

Although the more massive propane rocket requires more thrust than the hydrogen rocket, its pumps do not have to accommodate as great a volume flow. Moreover propane pumps are definitely easier to design than hydrogen pumps, even for the higher discharge pressure which is required. The main objection to the propane rocket is that the higher chamber pressure increases the amount of cooling to be accomplished, while propane is less effective than hydrogen as a gaseous coolant. Also, the specific impulse reduction resulting from film cooling is greater in the case of propane than in the case of hydrogen. However, propane, when used as a liquid coolant, is adequate.

Further improvements are possible in the choice of:

- Rocket fineness ratio
- Nozzle area ratio
- Thrust-to-weight ratio
- Propellant mixture ratio
- Trajectory shaping

Figure 11 shows that these gains will not be spectacular, however. At the same time, it shows that losses in these areas will not be crucial either.

An interesting feature of the single-stage rocket with a high initial acceleration is that engine shutdown occurs within line-of-sight range of the launch site. Even with throttling to a maximum acceleration of 4 g, the range for an eastward launch from South Point is about 350 kilometers, within optical sighting distance of both Mauna Loa and Mauna Kea. These two 13,500-foot mountains extend well above the clouds about 98 percent of the time.

Using comparable design criteria for a single-stage and a two-stage rocket, it turns out that because the first stage must support the second stage in a fully loaded condition during high acceleration, the mass fractions of both stages are approximately three times that for the single-stage hydrogen rocket. The advantages of staging are approximately cancelled by the high mass fraction, so that the simpler single-stage configuration seems preferable. There is more advantage in staging the propane rocket, but even here the advantage seems less impressive than the simplification which goes with the single stage.

Section 10

SUMMARY AND CONCLUSIONS

From orbit mechanics data now available (Refs. 1 to 7), it is possible to specify cargo mass requirements for all possible expeditions to Mars and Venus between 1960 and 1999. No one size fits all expedition requirements. The choice is also complicated by uncertainty whether propellant for the return trip can be manufactured from materials found on the planets. Because of the small number of rockets required for all inter- planetary and other solar space expeditions, a single size is dictated for all expeditions. It is found that a preliminary choice of 666 metric tons of cargo on earth parking orbit, mostly propellant for escape into hyperbolic orbit, is sufficient for some short stopover and all long stopover landing expeditions to Mars on the assumption that propellant must be carried there for the return trip. The same size cargo makes Venus landing expedi- tions possible, assuming a favorable environment there and assuming water for the manufacture of propellants. Fleets of two or three such masses can support short stop- over landing expeditions to Mars, even at times of near aphelion oppositions. In no case is rendezvous required on earth parking orbit, although rendezvous on earth park- ing orbit is not excluded, and may even be preferred.

Propellant selection is simplified by the comprehensive studies made during the past seventeen years in various places. Competitive elimination leaves a very brief list of possible choices. A final choice lies between oxygen-hydrogen and oxygen-propane.

To carry the same cargo, the propane rocket must be almost twice as massive, but only 0.90 times the height of the hydrogen rocket. Propane is selected because its use eliminates very costly installations which are required for the hydrogen rocket. These must be committed before extensive engineering is done on the hydrogen rocket, seven to eight years before the hydrogen rocket can be made operational, and with little oppor- tunity for subsequent revision. The launch mass of the propane rocket is 12,000 metric tons.

The rocket is single-stage to earth parking orbit. It is 20 m in diam. and 100 m tall.
It uses a plug-nozzle. It can be completely designed in the engineering office from
existing engineering knowledge. Reliability is achieved through rational design, and
planning of operations. If started now, the rocket could be operational for a rate of
twelve launches per year beginning in 1970.

Cost and schedule studies indicate that the rocket can be ready earlier than any competing rocket, at less cost, and with greater reliability and capability. Amortizing
the installation cost and practice-flight costs over the operational period of the rocket,
and adding the continuing overhead and unit cost, we obtain a cost of $450,000,000 per
year for twenty years beginning in 1970. This comes to $37,500,000 per launch attempt,
or $26 per pound of useful cargo on earth parking orbit. Of greater importance, how-
ever, is the fact that the broader and far more expensive national space program will
achieve manned landings on the planets several years sooner than appears otherwise
possible.

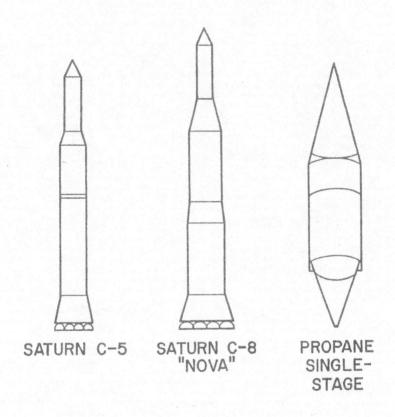

SATURN C-5   SATURN C-8   PROPANE
              "NOVA"   SINGLE-
                            STAGE

Fig. 2 Comparison of Rocket With Saturn C-5 and NOVA

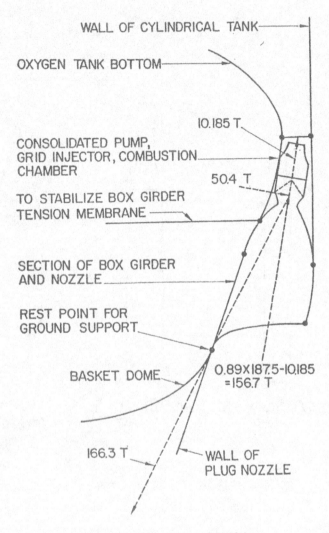

WALL OF CYLINDRICAL TANK

OXYGEN TANK BOTTOM

10.185 T

CONSOLIDATED PUMP,
GRID INJECTOR, COMBUSTION
CHAMBER

50.4 T

TO STABILIZE BOX GIRDER
TENSION MEMBRANE

SECTION OF BOX GIRDER
AND NOZZLE

REST POINT FOR
GROUND SUPPORT

BASKET DOME

$0.89 \times 187.5 - 10.185$
$= 156.7$ T

166.3 T

WALL OF
PLUG NOZZLE

Fig. 7 Schematic of One of 96 Motors

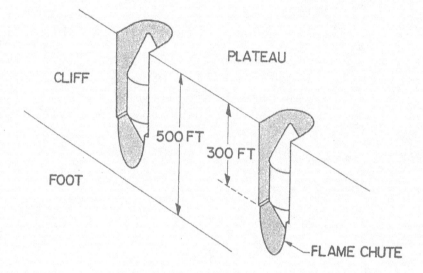

Fig. 14. Open Sided Assembly
and Launching Chimney

The Securities Biz

"There is a tide in the affairs of men, which taken at the flood, leads on to fortune. Omitted, all the voyage of their life is bound in shallows and in miseries."
William Shakespeare – Julius Caesar

I've always been haunted by that quotation. If only the magic moment had been seized. Fame and fortune would have followed. An old dream! If only you could go back and do it all over – knowing what you know now.

My tidal moment came in 1955. That's when I went to work for Auchincloss, Parker and Redpath (AP&R); Washington's most prestigious brokerage house. I knew nothing about the securities business; only that it had the reputation of being a glamorous business where the rich elites grew richer as in "Where are the Customer's Yachts?" AP&R was managed by Mark Sullivan, Jr; son of famed journalist Mark Sullivan, author of "Only Yesterday". I had walked in cold and asked for a job. Sullivan, probably having visions of Horatio Alger's "Ragged Dick" took me in off the street to be his assistant. I had never heard of Mark Sullivan or Hugh D. Auchincloss, the Standard Oil heir.

I had been raised in a home where the only books were the Holy Bible and an occasional Zane Grey novel. My father read the Grey; my mother the Bible, which she quoted with assorted Mondagraves. Nothing in the nature of history, art, music, let alone securities had ever been discussed in our home. I don't recall ever hearing an intellectual discussion in our home. Such a background did not prepare one to be Mark Sullivan's assistant.

Hugh D. (Hughdee) Auchincloss was AP&R's senior partner. In 1955, the great unwashed knew him only as Jackie Bouvier's step-father. AP&R was located at 729 15th St, NW. Mr Auchincloss occupied a lovely lead-glass fronted office looking down on 15th Street from the second floor. Mark Sullivan had a large office at the rear of the first floor with wall to wall, floor to ceiling windows. Sullivan was president of the Metropolitan Club and president of the Chevy Chase Country Club. He was also Chairman of the Board of Garfinckel Clothiers, who owned Brooks Brothers. AP&R had an active trading department and an Investment Advisory Department to manage the really big accounts. AP&R also managed the Atomic Development Mutual Fund (ADMF) which invested primarily in South African uranium companies. The mid-fifties uranium boom was in full swing.

But first, we need to get me there. I left my job at the Naval Gun Factory just before Washington's birthday in 1955. The gang at the office took me to lunch at the New England Restaurant on Maine Avenue. There were about a dozen excellent seafood restaurants on Maine Avenue. Washington was filled with fabulous restaurants before the Riots – Harvey's, Arnold's Hofbrauhaus, Duke Zieberts. Anyway, the temperature was in the 80s and we were in shirt sleeves. After lunch, it began to cloud up and get chilly. It started snowing about four o'clock. The snow was over a foot deep when my brother, Pug, drove Frank Hollowell and I to National Airport to catch the eight o'clock flight to Fort Lauderdale. Fort Lauderdale, called Liquordale, was the hottest town in Florida at that time. We were booked into the Escape, the hottest spot in Liquordale.

The Escape had great Calypso bands every night and a nine-hole pitch and putt course. Frank and I were chipping away and drinking beer, when we were suddenly confronted by two beautiful blondes. One was the Escape's social secretary; the other was a five foot two platinum blonde with ballerina legs and huge Bambi brown eyes – she was Dona! Dona invited us to a party at her family's apartment that night. Her family had rented the Escape's penthouse for the season and Calypso steel band for the evening. I don't remember the band's name but their most popular number was "Run Joe". Everybody tried their hand at playing a steel drum. Dona and I clicked. We spent the next day on the beach. She had just graduated from Sophie Newcomb, Tulane's sister school. Dona was intelligent, sophisticated, social and a bit spoiled.

She gave me her favorite "rubbing-rock". It was a smooth, concave little rock, that fitted neatly between the thumb and forefinger. I still have it. Dona later lived in a fabulous house in the French Quarter – 919 Dauphine Street. Dona later married a Charlottesville physician and lived in Farmington.

In 1955, AP&R had five young trainee brokers: Arthur Gardner, George Denby, Fred Menz, Bill Hulbert and me. Arthur Gardner's father was the Ambassador to Cuba at the time. George Denby's father was career State Department; his grandfather was the Secretary of the Navy during the "Teapot Dome Scandal". Fred Menz's family were Prussian nobility who had vast estates in East Germany. Fritz was married to Kathy Willard (Willard Hotel). She and her brother Henry still owned several blocks of F Street, NW between 9th Street and 15th Street. Hulbert and I were poor.

For some reason Sullivan and I experienced "a failure to communicate". I guess I expected him to actively teach me the intricacies of the business; sort of like a lecturer/coach. A mentor. Instead, he just let me sit at a desk by the door, like a gate keeper. He did assign me the task of setting the daily price of the Atomic Development Fund, which he had been doing. It involved multiplying the closing price of each stock by the number shares outstanding to get the net asset value, then adding the 8% load. It involved some convoluted calculations, which I quickly simplified. When I showed it to Sullivan, I'm not sure he was pleased. Sullivan affected an Ivy League British accent ala Dean Acheson, which occasionally provided comic relief. The accounting department was run by Harold Castro, who spoke with a heavy West Virginia hillbilly accent ala Chuck Yaeger. Sullivan opened the dialogue in his clipped British accent:

"Welle, Harolde, have you decided upon a new secretary yet?"
To which Harold replied in a Chuck Yaeger drawl:
"Yeah, Mark, I'm gonna hire the blond with the big tits."
On another occasion Bill Hoge reported the departure of his secretary to Sullivan:
"Well, Mark, Hannah is going to be leaving us this month".

Sullivan: 'Well, I'm certainly glad you're getting rid of that bitch".
Hoge: "We're getting married next month".

"Ragged Dicks" apprenticeship didn't work out. Sullivan and I failed to
develop a good working relationship. I had expected some sort of more
formal training program; I really don't know what Mark expected. At
any rate, I joined the other trainees all in a row outside Mr Auchincloss's
office. Hulbert, Edwards, Denby and Gardner, in that order. Denby was
helping to found the Hexagon Club, a theatrical group to stage annual
satirical political musicals. They were casting their first production.
Denby invited me to join up. Hexagon was a spectrum of types including
"Georgetown types" with clipped British accents. When pressed many
of the "Brits" were from places like Mauch Chunk, PA. Hexagon was
like UVA: party-party-party; some were black-tie. I asked my AP&R
associates if anyone knew where I could buy a new Tux cheap. Art
Gardner chimned in: "Jimmie, Louie's has very nice ones for $25;
that's where I get mine". Louie's was the DC outlet for Jos A Bank of
Baltimore. Arthur was right, they had Brook Brothers style and quality
clothes for "bargain-basement" prices. They were located on E Street
near the District Building.

Another nice thing about AP&R, they had a crew of interesting
secretaries. One, Pat, lived in a house full of beauties near "P Street
Beach" in Georgetown. They threw lots of parties. Across the back
fence was a house full of guys, who also threw lots parties. Howie
Simons lived in the house full of guys. I was invited to some of the
parties at both locations. That's how Howie Simons and I became
friends. Howie opened his first brokerage account with me. I started
him investing in Massachusetts Investment Trust (MIT), the most highly
regarded mutual fund in the industry at that time. We partied together
and became friends.

Howie was born in Albany, NY in 1929; he got his BA from Union
College in 1951; his MA in journalism from Columbia in 1952. He was
in the Cavalry in Korea. He became a science writer for several DC
news organizations; later he became editor of Science News. He joined
The Washington Post as a science writer in 1961. Howie was a gutsy
guy; he flew across the North Atlantic in a Piper Cub with Max Conrad.

The Post did a feature article about it in the Sunday Magazine section. Howie became managing editor of the Post in 1971. Howie married Tod Katz in 1967; they had four daughters. Howie was a great guy, laid-back, easy-going, great sense of humor. Howie's passions were science and technology, bird-watching, and fishing. We disagreed about politics, but we were both science and technology freaks.

We occasionally had lunch at a Chinese restaurant on Vermont Ave. near the Post. Nixon had just resigned. Ben Bradlee said Howie had "led the charge" on Watergate. Howie said: "What did you think about Nixon's resignation?" I said: "I think the Post just overthrew the government." We changed the subject. I'm ashamed to say I used to envy Howie; everything he touched turned to gold. One day at lunch, Howie told me about how taking care of a retarded child was driving Tod to a nervous breakdown. I never envied another person for the rest of my life.

Right after I finished building the prototype of the March Hare, Howie sent a reporter to my shop on Spring Hill Road in McLean. The Post did a half-page article on the car with an 6x9 picture of me sitting on the front fender. Howie left the Post to take a position as Curator at the Nieman Foundation for Journalism at Harvard. He died of pancreatic cancer while on leave from Harvard. I often think of Howie; he was a great guy.

The Auchincloss family always went to Newport for the summer and closed Merrywood, the family estate on Chain Bridge Road in McLean. Mr A opened up the pool at Merrywood to all AP&R employees. The summer of 1956, Mr A let me use his parking space in a garage on H Street just around the corner from AP&R. His secretary, Margaret Kearney sometimes gave me concert or show tickets he was not going to use. Mr A was an exemplar of noblesse oblige and the beau geste. He left Margaret a beautiful home on Bradley Blvd, next to the Chevy Chase Country Club.

I had an apartment on Cortland Place, across the street from the Kennedy Warren; my mother had an apartment at the corner of Connecticut and Tilden. After work, I would often stop by Mom's for a cup of tea. One afternoon in October 1956, when I knocked on the door, a wild-haired

lunatic answered. Mother had gone stark raving mad overnight. I
called my brother and we held her in bed all night. The next morning,
an ambulance took her to GW University Hospital. They put her in
a padded cell. Dr Groh diagnosed Schizophrenia and started shock
treatment. Later, she was transferred to St. Elizabeth's, the DC mental
hospital.

Up until then, mother had been able to take care of herself as a nurse.
Now, my brother and I had to pay off Dr Groh and take care of mother.
My brother, Pug, was doing well in the car business and was shouldering
most of the load. I was barely getting by at AP&R, so I started looking
around. Eric Ericson was AP&R's mutual fund liaison. Eric found out
Fidelity's "Gentleman Sid Weeden" was looking for an assistant; Eric
arranged a meeting . Sid and I immediately "clicked". Thus, I become
a "wholesaler".

Before departing AP&R, I need to mention three of the guys who became
good friends: George Denby, Fred Menz and Bill Hulbert. Denby was
born in Peking, China in 1929, son of James O. Denby, the U.S. Vice
Consul to Peking. His father was also born in Peking, the grandson of
Charles Denby, the first U.S. Minister to China. George and his brother,
Douglas learned Cantonese from their nurse. Aside from China, George
grew up in Ireland, Italy, Austria, and South Africa. George resembled
John Singer Sargeant's Lord Ribblesdale. George attended Le Rosey
School in Switzerland; the most expensive school in the world. "Rosey"
educated generations of Hohenzollerns, Rothchilds, and Metternichs.
He later attended Millbrook School and Princeton. He spent five
years in the U.S. Air Force, primarily in the Pacific Theater as Aide
to Commanding General Curtis LeMay. AP&R evolved into Prudential
Securities with Denby as Manager. He also became President of the
Chevy Chase Club and the Metropolitan Club. Douglas Denby became
President of the Association of American International Colleges and
Universities. George married three lovely ladies: Myrto Liatis, the Greek
Ambassador's daughter. Myrto was intelligent, fun, and tom-boyish; she
could whistle through her teeth like a man. Marion von Hagen Kober
produced two handsome sons; Douglas and Nichlos. Number three
Carmen Yoma, is a beautiful, intelligent, and fun Chilean. George's

parents had a 500 acre cattle ranch near The Plains, Virginia. The cattle kept breaking their legs in woodchuck holes, so Denby, Hulbert and I sometimes hunted "chucks" there. The ranch was edenic; lush woods and meadows among rolling hills. George and Carmen retired to Figure 8 Island near Wilmington, NC. George died May 7, 2014. George was a wonderful guy, great sense of humor, punctuated by a quiet chuckle. George was "sui generis".

Fred "Fritz" Menz was born in Germany; his family were Prussian nobility; we called him "The Count". His family moved to Washington when Fred was 12. They had a home near Lafayette Square and a summer "cottage" in Blue Ridge Summit, PA. Kathy Willard's family had a summer "cottage" nearby. Fred and Kathy were childhood friends. The "cottages" were palatial. To give you some idea of scale, at the rear of the entry hall at Fred's place was an enormous staircase, flanked by two porcelain urns about eight feet high and a meter in diameter. All furniture was huge and overwhelming . The bed posts in the guest room were about eight feet tall and sixteen inches in diameter. Kathy's place was on top of a beautifully landscaped hill. They belonged to a nearby golf club whose main attraction was that hardly anyone used it. They had two lovely daughters, Kathy and Vicky. Kathy was quiet and reserved like her mother. Vicki "sparkled" and she was gorgeous. Fred loved to drink and cook in no particular order; he was a gourmet cook. Weekends at the Blue Ridge were bacchanalian.

Fritz and I did the Oktoberfest one year. At a posh bar we ordered Martinis. When they arrived Fritz took one sip and started complaining about how after all these years these people still couldn't make a Martini. Actually, it was okay, but my "agent provocateur" side sensing an opportunity to see Fritz go ballistic, I agreed. Fritz called the kellner and began giving detailed instructions in fluent Deutsch. The waiter returned with a new batch. Fritz took one sip and exploded. Everyone in the bar were watching the "oper". Fritz dispatched the waiter with revised instructions. After a dramatic interval, while Fritz grew more agitated, the rapt audience witnessed the waiter pushing a serving cart toward our table. It had a silver bucket of ice, a bottle of Beefeaters, a bottle of Noilly Prat, a silver bowl of olives, a silver shaker, silver tongs, and fresh glasses. The kellner loudly relayed the bartender's message "fix your own verdammt Martinis!".

Bill Hulbert and I were buddies; our wives were friends. Bill and Pat were high school sweethearts; they had four sons. Bill and I were always trying to come up with some way to get rich quick. The Brazilians have a great soft drink, Guarana, which we tried to introduce here. We formed a company, the OBA! Corp; Oba! Is the Brazilian equivalent of Spanish Ole! We had cartons printed up and got a small bottler to run off a couple of thousand bottles. We planned to use Carnaval music in our ads. We tried to get grocery chains to try it. In the grocery business shelf space is every thing. Even if they open a little space, they expect you to give them the product - literally. It's a business that requires a lot of capital to break into, which we didn't have. We tried to start a mutual fund that would invest only in precious metals – The Elektrum Fund. Elektrum is the Greek word for an amalgam of gold and silver. Gold at that time was selling for $25 per ounce. A new fund was required to have $100,000 initial capitalization which we were unable to raise. You're probably beginning to get the picture. Anyway, we had fun trying. What Bill really loved was flying. At one point he took up soaring. Schweitzer built sail planes and taught soaring in Elmira, NY. Bill and I flew there. It is beautiful hill country with great thermals. Eagles fly formation with you. There are great watering holes in town. Bill has a pacemaker now and can't fly; it broke his heart.

II Louisburg Square

May 1957 had been a hot summer in Washington. Sunday I had had played golf in shorts and had sun-burned legs. Monday morning when I got off the plane in Boston, it was snowing. Sid Weedon, Fidelity's wholesaler for the Middle-Atlantic area, had hired me as his assistant and I was to report to the Boston headquarters for orientation. Raymond L. Myrer, President of Crosby Corp, Fidelity's sales organization, met me at the plane. Having no topcoat, I was destined to catch pneumonia my first day on the job.

Myrer drove me to his home, II Louisburg Square, to loan me one of his topcoats. Louisburg Square is on Beacon Hill and is one of the oldest and most expensive residential neighborhoods in America. It was horseshoe shaped with a park in the middle. Ray told me each house owns the section of park in front of their house. The houses were Greek Revival and posh inside and out. I was particularly impressed by the front doors. They were huge, about six inches thick, with huge sterling silver hinges, about a half-inch thick. Ray introduced me to his wife and gave me a "Cooks Tour". I don't know the 1957 prices, but currently, the houses are priced between $6 million and $20 million.

Ray drove us to Ye Olde Union Oyster House for lunch. It opened in 1826, the oldest restaurant in America; the building was older – 1704. It is located at 41-43 Union Street, on the waterfront. The toothpick was introduced in America at the Oyster House. It has large windows and large dark wooden booths. The food in traditional New England fare: fish, oysters, clams, lobsters, steaks, chops, poultry, and baked beans. I think I had a seafood platter. Outside, it was snowing. Inside, it was Christmas in May.

Ray talked about Fidelity and Christian Science, which was big in Boston. My mother was a disciple of Mary Baker Eddy, so I already knew about the "Keys to the Scriptures".

The Fidelity Fund was created in 1930. Boston lawyer, Edward C. Johnson II bought the fund in 1943, and turned it into a high performance stock fund. To balance the portfolio, he set up the Puritan Fund, the first income fund to invest in common stocks. Johnson was an innovator; he put individuals in charge of a fund, instead of committees. The earliest star of this approach was Gerry Tsai, a Shanghai immigrant he put in charge of the Fidelity Capital Fund in 1957. Ray introduced me to Edward C. Johnson II and the Fidelity staff, including Gerry Tsai. Edward C. Johnson II always wore a polka-dot bow tie.

Gentleman Sid Weedon

Sidney L. Weedon aka "Gentleman Sid" and "Dean of the Wholesalers" was Fidelity's wholesaler for the Middle-Atlantic territory (NY,PA,DE,MD,VA,WV). Fidelity had a sales charge of 8%; 6% went to Fidelity – 2% to Sid. New York City was the jewel in the crown. The Wholesaler was the public face of a fund; responsible for "Presentation". He wined and dined, coddled and cajoled the brokers in his territory, particularly the big mutual fund "producers".

Sid had been a Colonel in the OSS during WWII primarily liaising with the Brits as part of the "olde boy network". He was impeccable "Brooks Brothers" and always "correct" in demeanor. Sid was a mentor. He told me: "Jim, you never see the soles of a gentleman's shoes". Soon after reporting aboard, Sid took me on a training trip" through New York-- Albany, Buffalo, Syracuse. We traveled Club Car: Dark wooden paneling, overstuffed lounge chairs, elegant service by white-jacketed, white-haired, black waiters. Making our calls, we would check-in with the manager, chat with the top fund producers, then take a group of the "fund guys" to lunch or dinner at a posh restaurant. The best ''shops'' in the securities business attracted the "best people" who were often primarily managing their own or friends accounts. In Richmond, Bill Hulbert got his Michigan fraternity brother, Tom Howard, to introduce me to the "best people" in the business. Tom was one of "The Howards of Virginia". An FFV. Tom introduced me to people like Henry Valentine, another FFV. Henry's grandfather Edward, had been the most celebrated sculptor in America. Tom and I became buddies; he knew a lot of gorgeous Richmond women, who we sometimes entertained at his home. Tom and his brother Jim lived in a palatial home in Garden District. Jim went on to become the leading Constitutional Law professor at UVA.

In the fall, I met Sid in Charlottesville. He was staying at the Farmington Country Club, where he was a member. Saturday we went to Scotts Stadium for UVA's opening game. Sid always drove a new Cadillac. While we were driving around Charlottesville, he told me next year I would be able to afford one like his. Sunday evening he hosted a lavish dinner at Farmington for the top dealers in Charlottesville. Later in the

Fall, Fidelity had its annual meeting at the Harvard Club in Boston. Edward C. Johnson II introduced the attendees to his son Edward C. Johnson III, who had just joined the team. Eventually, the scepter was passed from II to III. He than proceeded to unveil Fidelity's long-range strategic plan. They had been secretly running number of funds in-house. They planned to go public with the ones that had performed best. Eventually, they planned to run a galaxy of funds designed to meet any customer objective. The customers loved it; the industry loved it. Johnson predicted enormous growth; he was right, Fidelity became the largest mutual fund company in the world. This was a truly historical meeting. It revolutionized the industry. All the major fund companies copied Fidelity and set up families of funds and funds of funds. The industry grew exponentially; from billions to trillions.

Every year, the mutual fund industry holds a national convention to show-off their wares to the retail brokerage industry. Each major fund rents a "hospitality suite" featuring a lavish bar and buffet. In 1957, the convention was held at the Statler in NYC. The fund's management and wholesalers serve as hosts. I was on duty at Fidelity's bar when Frank Batten and his blond-bombshell "secretary" visited our suite. Frank ran a very successful "bucket-shop" operation in Washington. Frank did not "hide his lamp under a bushel". He drove around downtown DC in a gold Cadillac convertible equipped with a loudspeaker which he used to invite girls to join him. All the brokers swarmed around Frank's "secretary" acting macho and "hitting" on her. Finally, one asked her: "How do you like the securities business?"
To which she replied: "Huh?"
He persisted: "How do you like working for a stockbroker?"
She turned to Batten in wide-eyed wonder and asked: "Are you a stockbroker, Frank?"
Batten replied: " Yeah, honey, I'm a stockbroker".

In view of Fidelity's golden prospects, Ed Johnson invited Sid to Boston to discuss a new contract. Sid told me Johnson said Sid would soon be making more money than he was making and wanted to cut his percentage from 2% to 1%. Sid would have soon been making more money than God. Sid flatly refused, saying a deal was a deal. I don't know whether Sid was fired or resigned. At a later meeting, someone said: "What about Jim Edwards?" Someone else said: "He's Sid Weedon's boy". Sid could have been the mentor I always needed.

Christmas 1956, had been a disaster, my mother was in St. Elizabeth's. In November, she had suddenly gone schizophrenic and spent weeks at GWU Hospital in a padded cell. A couple of days before Christmas 1957, I received a letter from the Crosby Corp. Before opening, I could see it contained a check. Assuming it was a Christmas bonus, my spirits soared. I remember thinking: "Well, Edwards, you've finally made it in the majors". It was from Ray Myrer, ending my Fidelity career on 12/31/57 and enclosing my severance pay. My contract with Fidelity was supposed to run until May. Fidelity was not faithful to their agreement. Alas, Christmas 1957 looked a lot like Christmas 1956.

I will close the way I began, with the Bard. Had my tidal moment been but seized, I would have had the know-how to implement some of the projects I later attempted. For example, in the early 1960s, I tried to start a New Technologies Mutual Fund. The timing would have been perfect and I don't believe anyone had such a fund at that time.

Gunfighter

Somewhere I had read an article about Gerry Bull and the HARP (High Altitude Research Project). It was a joint venture between McGill University (Gerry Bull) and Aberdeen Proving Grounds (Charlie Murphy). Ultimately, they planned to use large cannons as a low-cost way to launch payloads into Earth orbit. They had an elongated 16-inch cannon mounted at the end of the runway at Barbados airport. Lights started going off in my head about fantastic weapon system possibilities.

Vicki booked passage to Barbados on British West Indian Airways (BWI). This was a happy time when flying was a ball. As we approached BWI's plane parked on the tarmac at National we could hear vivacious Calypso music; as we boarded we were handed tall frosty rum punches. Before we got airborne, everybody on the flight was bombed.

We had booked into the Miramar Hotel, the first hotel constructed on the West Coast of Barbados. It had been built adjacent to the winter estate of Sir Edward Cunard, scion of the Cunard shipbuilding family. The Miramar is now named the Fairmont Royal Pavilion. The gardens are fabulous. I neglected to mention that Vicki was the assistant manager of Varig Airlines (The Brazilian Airline) in the Washington office. We had flown gratis on BWI and had a huge discount at the Miramar. Charlotte Franklyn was a good friend of Ruben Berta, the President of Varig Airlines. Charlotte, had been in charge of training Varig stewardess's in New York. She had a fabulous house on a hill near the St. James hotel area: Sandy Lane, Miramar, etc .

Gerry Bull was not on the island, but I arranged to see his right hand man – Dave Weiss. So, while Vicki visited her friend Charlotte, I went to the gun site. HARP had joined two smooth-bored 16"/50 naval cannons end to end with supporting structure at the joint. The last time anyone had built long-barreled guns like this were the WWI German "Paris Guns" (German name - Long Max), designed to fire 9-inch projectiles 70 miles to bombard Paris. The HARP gun was designed to fire straight up to an altitude of 100 miles. The current projectiles were Martlet 2Cs. Martlet 2Cs were fin-stabilized, sub-caliber rounds encased in sectional wooden canister sabots. The projectiles were 56-inches long, 5-inches in diameter, and weighed 200 pounds; the sabots were 16.450-inches in diameter and weighed 200 pounds. The sabots separated at the muzzle. The rounds were fired at muzzle velocity of 5000-6500 feet per second.

Gerry Bull and Charlie Murphy were a great team. Both were young geniuses, both had a great sense of humor, both loved to gossip, both loved aerodynamics, both detested bureaucracy. To illustrate this last point, a favorite story around SRI was about A.V. Roe and the Canadian Arrow. Canadian aircraft company A.V. Roe had developed the most advanced fighter aircraft in the world, the CF-105 Arrow, capable of Mach 2. A.V. Roe wanted to establish a strong Canadian aircraft industry. By 1959, four Arrows were flying and another eighteen were in production. There was growing interested abroad in acquiring Arrows. On 10/20/59, the Canadian House of Commons canceled the Arrow project and ordered the total physical destruction of all assets: all aircraft, tools, jigs, fixtures, drawings, and reports. This event had an enormous impact on Gerry Bull's attitude toward bureaucrats. Incidently, Gerry's motto was: " There is no tomorrow".

Dave Weiss and Carleton Braithwaite gave me a tour of the site. Dave was Bull's principal engineer and Carleton, who looked like Harry Bellafonte, was related to the prime minister of Barbados. Carleton was general manager of HARP Barbados. They assembled a Martlet 2C in the shop and showed me around the gun. At the end of the day Dave and Carleton gave me a ride back to Charlotte's house in a HARP Jeep. We spent most of our time in Barbados at the Sandy Lane. The Manager was a great Aussie bloke, Thomas R. Noonan, they had a great Calypso band.

My article "Long-Range Artillery" was published in the July-August 1964 issue of Ordnance Magazine proposing weaponization ideas based on HARP technology. I had no way of knowing at the time, but Gerry Bull and Charlie Murphy wanted me to do exactly that. The HARP charter did not permit them to do it. Jay Carsey worked at Naval

Propellant Plant (NPP), Indian Head, as assistant to Joe Browning, Technical Director and Al Camp, Chief of R&D. Jay took my article to Browning and Camp and suggested NPP get in the gun business. NPP made all the Navy's gun and rocket propellant and they made a profit on it. They had funds squirreled away for special projects.

Jay and I met at the Market Inn in DC and set the wheels in motion to transfer me from NASA, which they did in February 1965. They didn't have any room in the R&D Building at the time, so they put me in an abandoned barracks just outside the Main Gate. I had the building to myself, which I loved. I like working alone. I don't like committees. I think one or two dedicated men can accomplish more than a stadium full of committees.

My instructions were to weaponize the HARP technology; how I did it was up to me. My guiding principle is always KISS (Keep It Simple Stupid) and don't reinvent the wheel. To get started I needed to find out what had already been done and what every body was working on. So the first thing I had to do was get to know Gerry Bull and Co at McGill University and Charlie Murphy and Co at Ballistic Research Lab, Aberdeen Proving Grounds. I became a regular visitor at McGill, where I usually talked with Gerry Bull and Dave Weiss. At Aberdeen, it was Charlie Murphy and "Mac" MacAllister. All of them went all out to help me. Gerry took his own picture of the Barbados gun off the wall behind his desk and gave it to me. It hangs on the wall of my office at home.

Jay Carsey lived in a trailer behind an ESSO station, a few blocks outside the Main Gate. I would often stop in on the my to my barracks to share a cup of "Constant Comment Tea". Jay had been asked to take over the presidency of Charles County Community College (CCCC). He started working one day a week at NPP. Jay and I decided to name our baby "Project Gunfighter".

Someone downtown at the Bureau of Ordnance (BuOrd) decided NPP should demonstrate the technology. I found out Woody Saft at NWL Dahlgren had an experimental 5"/70 gun barrel stored on the

NWL range. I decided the quick and easy way to demonstrate the new technology would be to use the 5"/70 gun firing HARP 5-inch sub-caliber, fin-stabilized projectiles. I had Watervliet Arsenal smoothbore the 5"/70 and arranged to have 50 5-inch projectiles made by Aberdeen's supplier in Baltimore. I borrowed a 6"/47 mount for the 5"/70 from Saft, and shipped the whole lot to White Sands Proving Ground. There we planned to demonstrate range and dispersion.

In the interim, the TD had given Gunfighter a trailer next to the R&D Building. I had also been given some help. Jerry Temchin, Ken Songy, Steve Maxwell, and Bruce Kirk. Most valuable of all: Colonel Robert D. Heinl Jr, USMC, who could walk into almost any office in the Pentagon. He also wrote an internationally syndicated column on military affairs for the Detroit News.

The conventional 5"/54 gun's range is nine miles. We went to White Sands and broke the world record by firing the five-inch fin-stabilized projectiles to range of 75 miles. As a result, BuOrd decided they wanted a long-range projectile for the Heavy Cruiser (CA). The CA's 8"/55 gun has a range of 15 miles, BuOrd and USMC wanted a range of 40 miles to support amphibious landings. Gerry Bull formed a team composed of Dave Weiss and Frank Eyre to help us design the 8"/55 Gunfighter projectile. Eyre had worked on the Arrow project.

The Navy had reactivated New Jersey BB62 to give gunfire support in Vietnam. New Jersey's 16"/50s could not reach the Ho Chi Min Trail. Bu Ord asked us if we could design a projectile with a 50 mile range. I hit upon the idea of putting sabots on the Navy's stockpile of 12-inch projectiles from the extinct Battle Cruisers. Meanwhile, Bob Heinl found a stock pile of 23,000 280mm HE rounds for the Army's Atomic Cannon stored at Yuma Proving Grounds. Bob got the Army to consign the 23,000 rounds to Gunfighter. We designed a bucket type sabot like HARP's Martlet 2C sabot. Heinl named our 16-inch quick-fix the "Edwards System". The 16"/50 fired a 2500 lb. HE round to a range of 25 miles. Firing the 720 lb. 280mm round (shell 520 lb., sabot 200 lb.) the range was extended to 50 miles. Dispersion was a advantage firing at an area target like the Ho Chi Min Trail.

The Israelis adopted the system for their 175mm guns. The 175mm fired a standard 147 lb. round to a range of 35,000 yards . Placing a sabot on a 105 lb. 155mm round extended the range to 60,000 yards.

In May 1967, Gerry Bull submitted a proposal to the U.S. Government that might have shaped the outcome in Vietnam. It was titled: Application of H.A.R.P. Technology to Surface Bombardment at Ranges Up to 300 Miles. It proposed installing six to ten batteries of 16"/75s in Vietnam. They would fire three type of HARP projectiles , at a rate of one to three rounds per minute. They were:

Martlet 2G (sub-caliber, fin-stabilized), flight weight 380 pounds, range 250 miles, cost per shot $3000.
Martlet 2G-1 (sub-caliber, fin-stabilized), flight weight 1355 pounds, range 120 miles, cost per shot $7000.
Martlet 2H (full-bore, flip-out-fires), flight weight 2300 pounds, range 50 miles.
Terminal impact velocities 3000 feet per second (fps).

Batteries at Quang Tri could have covered Hai Phong harbor. Ten batteries firing just one round per minute, 24 hours a day, unaffected by weather, may have been too much for even Ho and Giap in the long run. It was not done, because just like Rollin Gillespie's proposals, Gerry Bull's were too advanced and too economical.

Dr. Gerald V. Bull was a remarkable man. He was born March 29,1928. He was the youngest man to receive a doctorate (aeronautical engineering) from the University of Toronto. At 33, he was the youngest full professor at McGill University. In 1954, he married petite and lovely Noemi (Mimi) Gilbert, daughter of Dr Paul Gilbert, who owned his own hospital in Churny, just across the St. Lawrence River from Quebec. Dr. Gilbert built Mimi and Gerry a palatial home in Churny. They raised five sons and two daughters.

After all the windows in Engineering Building were blown out by a light gas gun accident, a new off-campus lab site had to be found. With Dr. Gilbert's help, Jerry and Mimi had bought a tract of land at Highwater,

100 miles southeast of Montreal. It was Disneyland, hills and valleys covered in spruce and pine, remote, uninhabited and unspoiled. On top of the mountain , a giant triple A-frame, with vast expanses of windows on all sides were built. A swimming pool, tennis court, and ski lift were added. It evolved in to Space Research Corporation, a 10,000 acre laboratory and gun range. The horizontal 172 foot 16-inch gun fired research projectiles into a boxed canyon.

While promoting his Vietnam Supergun project, Gerry flew a party of industry and government heavy hitters to Highwater in a chartered Fairchild turboprop. The CO of Indian Head, Capt Leslie Olson and I were invited. The Triple A-frames were huge and all joined at the top with a roof that sloped to the ground. The middle one was one huge room that served as living room and dining room with a gigantic chandelier hanging down in the center. Here on an enormous table the Bull's had laid out an eye-candy smörgåsbord. Bubbly flowed like water; the guests had a great thirst. Olson was bug-eyed. The next morning, what was left of the attendees, were given a tour of the facility and treated to a special demonstration. The horizontal 16-inch gun was loaded with the largest charge tested to date. About 1200 pounds as I recall. No one knew if it was going to blow up the gun. We all watched with puckered assholes, like we were in minefield. The gun didn't blow, but it shook the country and sobered-up the attendees. We flew back to DC in the afternoon.

I had enjoyed working at AP&R. It had a crew of top-tiered likable men and a genteel atmosphere. However, the Gunfighter project was the only job I ever had where I couldn't wait to get to work in the morning.

The 8"/55 Gunfighter round we were now designing was a scaled-up, weaponized version of the HARP 5-inch projectiles we had fired at White Sands.

The final configuration of the 8"/55 Gunfighter round was:
Total shot weight 135 lbs, sabot weight 21.9 lbs, projectile weight 113 lbs.
Projectile length 54 inches, diameter 4.125 inches.

Muzzle velocity 4100 fps, Ballistic Coefficient 4500 lbs/sq.ft., G-load 21,700 Gs.
Range 40NM at a QE of 40°.

Five fins to maximize bore stability and enable a shorter sabot. The sabot is composed of three petals made of 7075T6 aluminum The sabot does not rotate, it is fitted with a brass slip-obturator. The fins chord form is wedge shaped with one face parallel to the shell axis to induce a slow roll rate, minimizing manufacturing misalignments.

We tested one of the projectiles in NWL Dalhlgren's Lethality Arena. A projectile was stood on its end in the center of a large circle of plywood panels. It was detonated and the fragmentation pattern of the fragments was mapped. Due to the elongated configuration of the Gunfighter shell it was found to be approximately equal to the standard 8-inch shell in lethality.

Meanwhile, unbeknown to me, Joe Browning had quietly sent Dom Monetta to SRI in Montreal to learn the HARP technology and ultimately take over Gunfighter. Alas, from the beginning, I had been playing the game on a "cloth untrue, with a twisted cue, and elliptical billiard balls".

Bob Heinl and I put in a lot of time making speeches and lobbying Navy and Marine Corps brass promoting Gunfighter. Bob was famous in the Corps; he had easy access to the top brass. The Marine Corps were our paramount supporters inasmuch as Gunfighter was primarily intended to provide gunfire support to the Marine Corps amphibious landing operations. Bob and I made numerous "social calls" on Corps brass. One day we visited a ledger-filled room in the bowels of the Pentagon occupied by a Marine "Bird Colonel". Unfortunately, I don't remember the good Colonel's name. Apparently, he functioned as the Marine Corps's comptroller. He was the man who allocated funds for the Five Year Plan. At Bob's suggestion he put Gunfighter in the plan for $5 million. My successors were credited with getting this big funding for Gunfighter, but it was really Bob and the Colonel. Unfortunately, Bob died shortly after writing "Written in Blood" and was not around to contest Indian Head's revision of history.

I reported our good fortune to my boss, Al Camp, Chief of R&D. He said I could look forward to being promoted to GS-15 inasmuch as my budget would be larger than his. This development obviously threw a wrench into the TD's long-range plans. Joe Browning (TD) had a group of favorites on station called "Joe's FHBs-Fair-Haired-Boys". I was not a member. This triggered a Memorandum dated 28 February 1968:

- Subj: New Managerial Senior Staff Assignments
- Effective 4 March, Martin A. Henderson will become Manager of our principal Gunfighter project, the 8"/55 fin-stabilized system.

James B. Edwards will become our principal full-time planner for all other long-range-gun programs - - -"

My leg's had just been chopped off at the neck. Marty was a nice guy, but he had not worked one day on any facet of Gunfighter. I now had no project, no staff, and no prospects of promotion. I was told the management hoped I would "find a new Gunfighter project". This raised a lot of eyebrows around DOD.

Bob Heinl got me assigned to a 'blue-ribbon' panel of admirals, captains, and colonels called the Amphibious Warfare Concepts Study at NRL Anacostia. They were researching 21st Century Amphibious Warfare. I was charged with Future Gunfire Support Systems. My co-worker was Colonel David R. Griffen, a friend of Bob Heinl. Captain George Hutchinson (Hutch) was in command. Admiral R.H. Phillips and Colonel D.J. Decker were on board representing B-K Dynamics. B-K Dynamics was owned by a friend of mine Ira Kuhn.

I had come up with concept of a new class of Landing Force Support Ship (LFS) equipped with 12"/70 guns firing full-bore, fin-stabilized, rocket-assisted guided projectiles to a range of 190 NM. I had been working on it as Gunfighter's next project while I was still the Manager. None of my successors came up with any significant advances in gun system technology.

Hutch took the panel to Newport, RI for a presentation to the Naval War College. While there, I toured some of the "cottages" and had a drink with Cdr. Ed Beach, author of "Run Silent, Run Deep". He was a friend of Captain Dan Carrison a member of the panel. We later made the same presentation at NWL Dahlgren. My section on the 12"/70 received a standing ovation. Captain Olsen and several NOSIH people were there, but none came over to congratulate me afterward. I had apparently already disappeared down Orwell's "memory hole".

Not seeing any prospects for the future, I resigned from NOSIH. Dom Monetta was appointed manager of Gunfighter and was promoted to GS-15.

There could have been a rosier scenario.

In 1968, Gerry Bull was looking for a buyer for the Space Research Corp. Renato had the vast resources of ITAU at his disposal. Bull would have leaped at the chance to move SRC to Brasil. Brasil could have become the World leader in gun technology. Renato and I could have set up a company to manage the whole operation. Gillespie left NASA in 1969. There is an excellent chance he would have leaped at the prospect of making Brasil a World leader rocket technology.

HARP-Barbados

5"/70 - Carsey, Kirk, Edwards, Songe

Songe, Temchin, Edwards, Olsen, Carsey, Kirk

CONFIDENTIAL

PROPOSED TECHNICAL APPROACH

LONG-RANGE BOMBARDMENT ROUND FOR

8"/55 NAVAL GUNS

JANUARY 1968 (1st Rev.)
(Supersedes March 1967 Submission)

Naval Ordnance Station

Indian Head, Maryland

CONFIDENTIAL

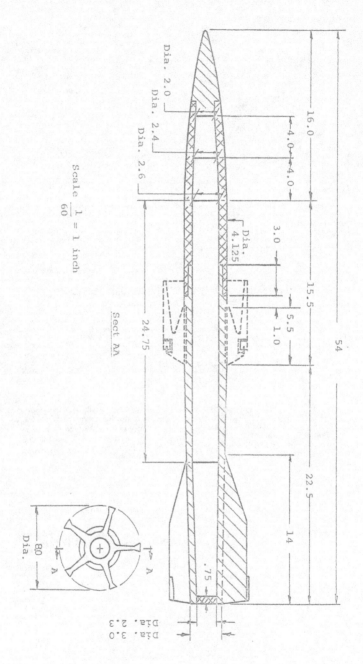

The Shell Structure

FIGURE 3

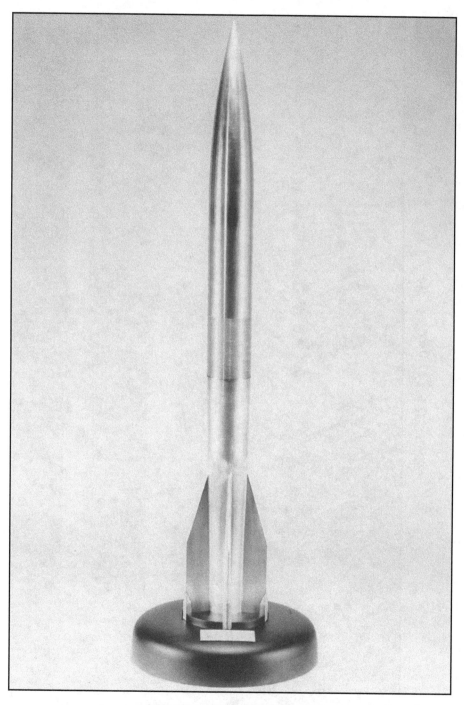

8"/55 Gunfighter Projectile

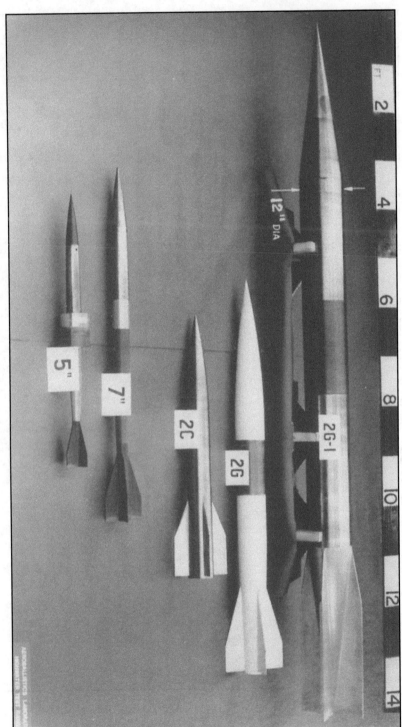

Fig. 6- Array of HARP Missiles

Department of the Navy

COMMENDATION
for

SUPERIOR ACCOMPLISHMENT

Official Recognition

to

James B. Edwards

for

Sustained Superior Performance

Presented on this 4th day of May 19 67

LESLIE R. OLSEN, Captain, U. S. Navy
Commanding Officer, Naval Ordnance Station
Indian Head, Maryland

Col. Heinl reports

Navy cannon may eclipse rockets

THE DETROIT NEWS—Thursday, Jan. 9, 1969

By COL. R. D. HEINL, JR.
Detroit News Military Analyst

WASHINGTON—In an era when the missile, bomb, rocket and high-performance aircraft are the glamor weapons, the old-fashioned gun, both afloat and ashore, is in process of an unheralded breakthrough with profound military implications.

Under the code name Project Gunfighter, the U.S. Navy has for the last three years been conducting a series of developments in gun and ammunition design which, experts say, may result in the greatest single advance since the invention of rifling.

In Project Gunfighter the Navy has been firing experimental projectiles with engineering accuracy at ranges so great that the normal gunnery proving grounds of the Army and Navy cannot be employed. Test shots have instead been fired using National Aeronautics and Space Administration (NASA) facilities at White Sands, N.M., and in the ranges at Wallops Island, Va., and Barbados.

BASED ON WHAT is known as the "Edwards system"—taking its name from inventor J. B. Edwards, a NASA engineer and now employed by the Navy Department—the project embodies ultra-high-velocity ammunition and projectiles of new design, combined with other features that enable these components to be fired through existing guns without modification.

In general, gun and artillery development has been a moribund field since before World War II. After the war, when advances could logically have been expected, the rocket and missile—scientifically glamorous, expensive, and seemingly of unlimited potential,—usurped the attention of scientists and engineers to the exclusion of the workaday gun.

Advances in metallurgy, propellants chemistry, aerophysics, and other scientific fields, have not seriously been applied to gun or artillery design in many years.

The Navy's present 8-inch gun, on the bulk of our cruisers, was designed in the early 1930s, thus representing the most advanced ballistics engineering of World War I.

While, to be sure, both the range of a $35,000 missile can out artillery and gun designs not many — the underlying technology still dates from the 1930s or earlier.

Now that the Edwards system is a reality, with test firings well advanced in at least two calibers, the enormous cost disparities between the economical, reliable, cost-effective gun and the dazzlingly expensive, militarily untried missile are being highlighted.

IN ONE application of the Edwards system (to the Navy 8-inch gun) it appears that a projectile with nearly the range of a $35,000 missile can be produced for a little over $1,000.

Using a modified Navy 16-inch gun, McGill scientists a crash effort be made to produce Edwards ammunition for fired 15-inch shells a hundred miles straight up. From knowledge gained in this project, Edwards was able to propose military applications now bearing his name.

WITH SUPPORT and funding from Rear Adm. Arthur R. Gralla, head of the Navy's Ordnance Systems Command, one of its original boosters, the Edwards system is being closely watched in all the services.

If it continues to live up to expectations, those who have sar

Mexican Red Cross urges 'peace day'

GENEVA—(AP)—Jose

The Army-McGill efforts witnessed experimental firing dating from the late 1960s were believe that Project Gunfighter will be a milestone in ordnance technology.

It was urged originally that a crash effort be made to produce Edwards ammunition for the Vietnam debut of the battleship New Jersey, but factions in the Navy opposed to recommissioning the battleship gave top priority to other aspects of the program.

Much of the basic research from which Edwards, an Ordnance Systems Command, developed the system stems from work originally conducted by the Army in connection with McGill University in Montreal.

COL. HEINL

Egyptians confronted by Israeli superguns

By COL. R. D. HEINL JR., USMC (Ret.)
News Military Analyst

WASHINGTON — If the Egyptians launch their much-bruited cross-Suez attack into the Sinai Peninsula, as Anwar Sadat has threatened and as some analysts have forecast they will, one Israeli surprise to greet them will be the longest-range field gun in the world.

Applying a highly advanced range-extension system, developed experimentally in the United States, to the U.S. Army's long-barreled 175mm gun, Israeli ordnance engineers have produced a weapon reportedly capable of hurling a 105-pound shell to a range of 60,000 yards, or roughly 34 miles.

Col. Heinl

The tactical significance of this tremendous capability is that Israeli gunners can cover attempted Suez crossings with artillery fire from positions far beyond the range of any of Egypt's Russian-model heavy artillery. They likewise can shoot counterbattery missions with impunity against Egyptian guns deep inside their opponents' lines on the other side of the moribund canal.

WHAT THE ISRAELIS have done, according to ordnance specialists, converts the 175mm gun — considered something of a turkey by U.S. artillerymen in Vietnam — into a species of supergun ideally suited to Israeli's defense requirements in the Sinai.

The nominal range of the self-propelled long gun with U.S. ammunition is more than 35,000 yards and it is that figure (about 20 land miles) that Israeli publicity attributes to the 175mm guns — probably an eight-gun or 12-gun battalion, obtained last year from the United States.

By modifying a lighter weight, smaller 155mm high-explosive shell so that it can be fired with supervelocity powder through the 175mm gun, the range of the weapon is said to have been increased more than 50 percent.

Even with the trade-off between the normal 175mm projectile, weighing 147 pounds, and the 105-pound 155mm shell, the results are well worthwhile, as anyone knows who ever has come under fire from 155mm (or the Russian equivalent, 152mm) artillery.

IT IS SOMEWHAT ironic that the Israeli development being hailed for its innovation is in fact part of a system successfully developed for the U.S. Navy, tried during the latter part of the Vietnam war and finally shelved due to Navy disinterest in the gun and its technology. While the Israeli variation employs spin stabilization of the lighter weight shell (as compared with the Navy's use of stabilizing fins), both techniques comprise part of what is called the Edwards system.

Conceived by James B. Edwards of Arlington, Va., the system that bears his name and which the Israelis seemingly have adopted enabled the 40-year-old eight-inch guns of USS St. Paul to deliver accurate fire against North Vietnamese shore targets 40 miles distant — the longest-range artillery firing on record since that by the Germans' 1918 Paris guns, nicknamed "Big Bertha."

The Edwards system also was tried with considerable success as a means of experimentally extending the range of the U.S. eight-inch howitzer but again was shelved, this time because of competition from a rocket-assisted ammunition system.

ADOPTION OF Edwards-design ammunition by the Israeli defense forces will have the practical effect of keeping the concept active, will afford field testing and ultimately may impart to this American-developed idea something of the belated modishness gained by the famous Christie tank suspension, offered in vain by its inventor to the U.S. Army during the 1920's and snapped up by Russia instead.

The Israelis, who were the first to point out that a prophet is not without honor save in his own country, thus may have applied that point equally well to American ordnance.

SPACE RESEARCH INSTITUTE
OF
McGILL UNIVERSITY

2 November 1966

Leslie R. Olsen
Captain, U. S. Navy
Commanding Officer
U. S. Naval Propellant Plant
Indian Head, Maryland
20640

Dear Captain Olsen:

Thank you for your letter of 13 October and your kind
comments on your visit. We sincerely hope that a close working
relation will develop with the Navy.

I am most pleased to pass the following comments regarding
my impressions of Jim Edwards. As you are aware, we have seen
him considerably since the start of your Gunfighter Program.
It is our opinion that he has done a first rate job as project
engineer on the program. He has performed well, all the functions
expected of a project engineer; such as, the collection and
evaluation of systems performance, the planning of program
tests, and the direction of technical effort. I have no
hesitation in recommending him most highly on the basis of
this performance.

We will look forward to further visits.

Yours sincerely,

G. V. Bull,
Director

GVB/lt

TO WHOM IT MAY CONCERN:

I have known Jim Edwards for almost two years.
During this time I have had numerous lengthy technical
discussions with him covering virtually all aspects of
our respective programs. In the course of our relationship
I have come to recognize him as the Navy's principal
authority in the field of long range gun systems, and have
dealt with him as a professional engineer of high competence
and maturity.

LEONARD C. MacALLISTER
Deputy Chief
Free Flight Aerodynamics Br.
Exterior Ballistics Laboratory
U. S. Army Ballistics Research
Laboratories

Julian (Jay) Nance Carsey

I met Jay when he recruited me to go to Indian Head in February 1965 and start the Navy's super gun program. Jay had a degree in chemical engineering from Texas A&M. He went to work at Indian Head in 1958 and worked his way up to assistant to the Technical Director and the Chief of R&D. He also taught math at Charles County Community College (CCCC) at night in an abandoned Nike missile site. In 1965, they made him their first president, the youngest Community College president in the U.S. Under jay's administration, CCCC grew exponentially. A college president is supposed to find money – Jay was a wizard. Jay was one of the nicest guys you'll ever meet; everybody in Charles County knew and liked him, they called him "Uncle Jay".

In 1965, Jay lived in a trailer behind Dick Fuch's ESSO station, a few blocks outside NPP's main gate. He usually dined at a greasy spoon called Charley's Diner. I would often stop by Jay's on the way to work to share a cup of "Constant Comment". Jay's life-style changed dramatically when he married Nancy Brumfield. They bought an apartment at Watergate, a cottage on the Chesapeake named Marchosa, and finally Green's Inheritance. It was a 23-room mansion right out of "Gone with the Wind". A long tree-lined road led from the gate to the mansion. A large formal dining room was dominated by a full-length, life-sized oil portrait of Nancy. The Carsey's threw frequent and lavish parties of 100 to 200 guests. Every weekend was a frantic whirlwind of parties, concerts, theater, dinners. They traveled extensively.

Jay had performed a miracle at CCCC. He was a great organizer and manager. He told me he needed only two or three days a week to run CCCC. The road seemed open to becoming a Congressman of Senator. The College paid Jay a good salary and gave him a housing and entertainment allowance for Green's Inheritance. College groundkeepers took care of GI's grounds. Jay made more than his college salary from consulting. Jay formed a corporation, Camelot, that put in roads and subdivided GI's 188 acres. Jay reportedly made over a million dollars on the deal. But he could never keep up with Nancy's expenditures. As Jay's friend, Dom Monetta said: Nancy was "always ten percent above whatever financial level they were at, no matter what level. So if Jay was making a million dollars a year, or even ten million, Nancy would always find a way to acquire bigger and bigger things. If Jay made ten billion dollars a year, she would be refitting the battleship New Jersey and making it a private yacht".

All this was destroying Jay, in his own words: - - - "once you've gone around the world three times, gone on every goddamn cruise ship, traveled first-class, stayed at the Plaza in New York and the Savoy in London – we never stayed anyplace else – once you've done that sort of thing, you've done it, and you acquire all this crap, you've got houses full of it - - -".

The above and following quotes are from "Exit the Rainmaker" by Jonathan Coleman, which provides a detailed description of the disintegration of the Carsey's marriage.

Nancy controlled, dominated, and regularly humiliated Jay publicly. Conversely, he had no control of her. The Dean, John Sine visited Marchosa one Saturday morning to see Jay. Nancy was getting ready to go play golf and had lost her golf shoes. She was screaming lurid obscenities at Jay for not helping her. Then she shifted the barrage to Sine for just sitting there doing nothing. Never one to back away from a confrontation, Sine stood up and said: "Hey, lady, you've got a license to tell him what to do, but with me you've got nothing".

Jay was a New Republic style "liberal". He was a strong supporter of the New Republic's idea of having the government pay every citizen a "living wage". A large number of Texas A&M "Aggies" worked at White Sands: crew-cut, gung-ho patriot types. Jay, an ex-"Aggie", ridiculed them. I think he had turned his back on the "Aggie" credo. When Jay and I traveled together to places like White Sands or China Lake, he didn't drink anymore than I did. The only time we ever got drunk was on a flight from Dulles to Los Angeles (we were going to China Lake). The plane had developed some kind of mechanical problem, so we had to return to Dulles. We spent about an hour circling Northern Virginia, dumping fuel. Jay and I were sitting across the aisle from a group of soldiers – one was named Orville Sleath. We could see his name tag. Jay and I were downing martinis; the more we drank, the more hilarious the name became. When Jay disappeared I was sure he had gone to Alice Springs and become Orville Sleath. Later, Jay told me he had toyed with the idea.

On Wednesday, May 19, 1982, Jay parked the College's black Caprice Classic at National Airport, put the keys in the glove compartment, left a copy of New Yorker on the seat, dropped six letters and post card in the mail box. He bought two expensive suitcases, checked-in, made his way to Pan Am's Clipper Club, and started putting away Vodka Martinis. Within an hour, Jay had vanished into thin air. A couple of days later, Jay's letters started arriving in Charles County.

Louis Jenkins, chairman of the college's board of trustees, received Jay's letter of resignation:
Louis -
Effective 15 May 1982 I resign as President. I am proud of what I have accomplished but its time for new leadership.
J. N. Carsey

The Dean, John Sine, got a postcard. Jay had played the lead, and John had directed Potomac Players production of "The Rainmaker". John's postcard read:
John -
Exit the Rainmaker. Good luck.
Jay
pls handle

Nancy received two notes. One a brief goodbye, telling her to listen to a tape in his desk. The other, an un-notarized note leaving the estate to her.

The New Yorker magazine Jay had left on the seat of the College's car was open to a cartoon on page 29. The cartoon showed a couple at their kitchen table. The wife was drinking coffee. The man was standing by the table wearing a suit and hat and carrying a brief case, there were two suitcases at his feet. He was saying: "Well, good bye, Emily. It's May 19th. You may remember my having mentioned some time ago that I was going to leave you on May 19th".

Jay's mysterious disappearance was the leading topic of conversation in Charles County. The regulars at the Hawthorne Country Club lamented: "If only Jay had chartered a plane, we could have all gone".

Jay ended up in El Paso, not as Orville Sleath, but as Jay Martin Adams. At first, he lived in a $160 per month room at the Y. He booked a lot of time at Moriarity's bar-restaurant and the more bohemian Back Door nearby. He met Dawn Garcia shooting pool at the Back Door. Dawn Garcia stood about five feet, was brunette, pretty, feisty and bright. She was head of the city's Department of Aging. She and Jay started going together. Later, Jay bought TJ's Bar and Grill at 5810 Dyer Street; he lived in an apartment upstairs. Eventually, the regulars at TJ's Bar discovered Jay Martin Adams was Julian Nance Carsey. The Washington Post had done a front-page piece on him. In the September 27 issue of People magazine, with Princess Grace on the cover, the feature article was about Jay. After Jay and Nancy finally divorced, Jay and Dawn married. They signed on for a program that sent teachers to overseas Air Force bases to teach graduate courses. They went to Lakenheath AFB near Cambridge University. I stayed with them for about a week. There are thatch-roofed villages everywhere, each with an ancient Pub. The clientèle were horsey country squire types – the atmosphere thick enough to slice. The Pub we frequented in Cambridge was often filled with members of the cast of "A Piece of Cake".

One of Jay's favorite words was "hecticity" as in hectic. I believe the "hecticity" of life at Green's Inheritance was at odds with his basic nature. I'm sure he enjoyed the "Carnaval" and prestige for awhile. But Nancy's unending extravagance kept him with his back to the wall. And the "manic" activity grows thin with time. The last time I talked to him, he said his life now was very different, very quiet, and he loved it. By nature, he was a quiet, laid-back, likable guy.

Jay was happy as a clam about their digs at Watergate. He met me in the garage, elating about never having to shovel snow again. We toured the court yard where there were shops to meet your every need: grocery store, drugstore, liquor store, dry cleaners, barber shop, flower shop, bakery. The bakery was fabulous, Vicki and I used to come over from Arlington to shop there. There was a mall with an excellent restaurant, and posh boutiques like Gucci's. In the lobby of their building, Watergate South, was one of DC's best eateries – the Merry-Go-Round. Their condo had a balcony with a great view. Nancy had furnished it beautifully. The Kennedy Center was across the street. Jay was intrigued with the idea that you could live your life there. Nancy was less sanguine. This discontent ultimately led to Green's Inheritance. The last time I saw Jay he was back in El Paso working at UTEP. He was in DC on business and he called me. We had lunch at our old watering hole the Market Inn. We talked about the old days and what happened to who. He told me Joe Browning had died. Later, Jay left UTEP and Dawn and ended up in Jacksonville teaching math and public administration at local community colleges, the last being St. Leo College. Jay spent his last seven years living quietly with his lady Corine Silverton near Jacksonville. I had planned to stop of to see them on my winter trips South, but something always came up. Jay sent a picture of himself on their patio shortly before he died in August 2000. He was 65.

I still remember the happy-go-lucky guy who lived behind the ESSO station.

Robert Debs Heinl Jr
(1916-1979)

Born in Washington, DC; related to serial Socialist candidate for president, Eugene Debs.
Graduated from Yale University in 1937.
U.S. Marine Corps 1937-1964; retired as Colonel.
Married Nancy Gordon; they had a daughter named Pamela.

The Heinl's lived at 2300 California St, NW, in the midst of most of the world's embassies. The house was lovely inside and out; the garden beautiful.

Bob was on duty at Pearl harbor on December 7, 1941. He was in combat on several islands, including Iwo Jima. He was on the team that took over Chichi Jima after the war. Chichi Jima was much more heavily fortified than Iwo Jima and had enough food and ammo to hold out for years. Notwithstanding ample rations, the Jap officers of Chichi Jima dined on exotic dishes composed of prisoners. There was a post-war book about it: "The Cannibals of Chichi Jima". President George H.W.Bush was shot down near Chichi Jima. In 1952-1953, Heinl commanded the defenses of the UN held islands facing the North Korean fortress city of Wonsan. Hundreds of rounds of artillery were exchanged daily between Wonsan and the artillery-studded islands under Heinl's command. Heinl's island forts were supported by myriad warship classes up to the battleships New Jersey and Wisconsin.
Heinl wrote a nationally syndicated column about military affairs for The Detroit News. He was recognized as one of the top military analysts in the world. He was one of the founders of the Heritage Foundation.
He was a prolific writer:
Marine Officers Guide
Handbook for Marine NCOs.
Soldiers of the Sea: U.S.M.C. 1775-1962.
Dictionary of Military and Naval Quotations.
Victory at High Tide: The Inchon-Seoul Campaign.
Written In Blood: The History of Haiti.

The Marine Corps were the principal supporters of the Gunfighter Project. Bob came onboard Gunfighter in 1965 to be our liaison to the Corps. Bob had easy entree anywhere in the Navy. He knew everyone; everyone knew him. He and I made many team presentations. We made a lot of "social calls" on Corps brass. One day we visited a ledger-filled room in the Pentagon occupied by a lone Marine Colonel. Unfortunately, I don't recall his name, but somehow Nate Smith rings a bell. I think he functioned as the Marine Corps's comptroller. He was the man who allocated funds for the Five Year Plan. At Bob's suggestion, he put Project Gunfighter in the Plan for $5 million. After we left the room, Bob said: "Gunfighter just got five million bucks". My successors at Indian Head were heralded for getting the big funding for Gunfighter, but it was really Bob and the Colonel.

The Detroit News offices were in the National Press Club building. Bob had a roll-top desk just like W.C. Fields. Fields could carefully reach into a yard high stack of papers and extract a small slip of paper with the relevant data - so could Bob. Bob and I often sought the elusive "perfect Martini" at the National Press Club or the Army and Navy Club. There were many intrepid searchers at both locations. Having Howie Simons, Sam Butz and Bob as friends permitted frequent sojourns at the Press Club. There were more serious drinkers per square yard there than any place in town.

Bob and Nancy loved sailing; they kept a day-sailer in Annapolis. To celebrate the publication of "Written in Blood", they were sailing the Caribbean on a schooner when Bob had a stroke and died in 1979. In Nancy's words: "Death as he would have wished, came swiftly, on a beautiful beach in the Caribbean. Only it came too soon. Even when life seemed darkest,, Bob wanted to live to be a hundred, always with the proviso that he be of sound mind and relatively sound body. There were more books to write, more causes to champion, more places to explore - - - .

"Beyond that last blue mountain barred with snow. Across that angry or   glimmering sea".

Jesse Sam Butz, Jr

Sam was born and raised in Jacksonville, Florida. His father was the Managing Editor of the Florida Times-Union. After graduating from high school in 1946, joined the Army and became an instructor at the Fort Benning, Georgia Airborne School. Their football team the "Doughboys" won the National Service championship. Sam was a tall rangy athletic man with the friendly easy-going nature large men usually have. In 1952, he graduated from the University of Florida as an aeronautical engineer. From 1952 to 1955, he worked for McDonnell Aircraft Company in St. Louis. Between 1955 and 1957, Sam worked with Arthur Kranish writing the newsletters: Bioastronautics Report and Washington Science Trends. Kranish was a very good friend of Howie Simons, which is how Sam came to know him. Between 1957 and 1960, Sam was Technical Editor of Aviation Week. From 1960 to 1973, he as with Air Force Magazine. In 1964, Sam and I wrote articles proposing weaponizing the HARP technology. I wrote mine for Ordnance Magazine. After I became manager of Project Gunfighter in 1965, we met for lunch to discuss the coincidences of our articles and became good friends.

Sam's work at Aviation Week and Air Force required that he visit aircraft and space industry facilities all over the world. One trip was to the Soviet Union in the middle of the winter. As was SOP, Sam had an Intourist "guide", a KGB man assigned to stick to him like glue. The KGB man was a big red headed guy who looked like an NFL lineman. He didn't like Sam and wasted no opportunity to show it. In the "Worker's Paradise", food was always in short supply and the comrade citizens went to any length to get it. Thus, all trains and planes were packed with people desperately clutching bags and boxes of every kind of food: potatoes, onions, cabbage, apples, whatever. By Western standards, the food was one step above garbage: tiny spotted potatoes, apples, etc. There was a blizzard raging and Sam and his "guide" were standing in the plane door ready to board. Back in the line, a Russian grandmother, a 'Babushka", with the signature white scarf tied round her head, had dropped her string-bag of potatoes, which spilled all over the tarmac. While her comrade countrymen ignored her plight, she desperately tried to recover her treasure. The plane was reving its engines and the other passengers scrambled to get on board. Sam ran out and began helping the "babushka" gather her tiny potatoes; the KGB man rushed out to help them. From that point on the KGB man treated Sam like he could walk on water.

Sam married his high school sweetheart, Susan, whose family owned a large farm near the Jacksonville airport.   Later, when the airport expanded, Susan became quite rich.   Hood and Carolyn Roberts were their best friends from high school. Hood had a repertoire of thousands of jokes and could keep a room full of people in hysterics for hours. Hood was in charge of Linguistics/computer studies at American University. Hood said that what was needed to integrate computers and linguistics was a team of 20 geniuses like Einstein and Galileo. Carolyn ran a legal update service on M Street, NW. From 1980 to 1993, Sam was technical analyst at the CIA; they called him the "AvWeek mole". Sam and I had another writing coincidence. In 1991, while I was writing "The Great Technology Race", about 21st Century technologies like nanotechnology and robotics, Sam was writing the same kind of report for the CIA.

The March Hare

After doing a good job at Fidelity and an outstanding job at Indian Head and receiving a royal screwing in payment, I decided to go into business for myself. Pumas were selling like Pinga in Brazil and Kit Kars like hot cakes in the States, why not hop on the Carrozzeria band wagon? It seemed like a good idea at the time!

Fiberfab was the "Top Banana" in the Kit Kar game so I booked passage to see Mike Aggeler, the plant manager in Santa Clara, CA. Mike was a big pleasant guy who loved to tell tales about the industry. Fiberfab had been founded by a guy named Warren (Bud) Goodman in 1964. He successfully built Fiberfab into number one in the industry. Then, one morning, he leaned across the breakfast table and shot his wife between the eyes with a .347 Magnum – he found out she was cheating on him. He told about how Fiberfab had gotten a set of molds of a new show car. They had secretly put a crew of fiberglass experts in the van that was carrying the car to an auto show. In transit, the guys took a "splash-mold" of the car; the owners never found out how it had been copied.

Mike suggested I visit Thermodynamic Systems. They were building a revolutionary tiny but powerful engine. A fellow named John Marshall was building a sleek car to mount it in. I got to know John ; asked him to design a car for me. Thermodynamics folded and John went back to BYU to head up the Design School. I started to look for someone to build the full-scale model of the car – the plug. The plug was used to make the molds. Peter Van Dine was building the most beautiful sailboats in the Annapolis area. I asked him to build the plug and molds for my car. He was too busy, but he told me about Leavenworth (Worth) Holden. Worth had been in charge of Trumpy Yachts loft. Trumpy had built the most elegant yachts in America. Just to give you an idea, its deeply recessed portholes were lined with gold leaf. Trumpy had been located in Eastport, just across the Severn River from the Naval Academy. They went out of business because John Trumpy would not build fiberglass boats.

Worth Holden was a gentleman. He was also an artisan, an antique restoration cabinet maker and ocean sailor. He was white-haired, slim and wiry, soft spoken and droll. He and his lovely wife, Kay, lived in a pretty house in Eastport. John Marshall and I had been designing the car by mailing drawings back and forth and talking on the phone. John invited me to visit him in Provo to finalize the design. Mormons are very active socially, they seem to have some kind of "eatin-meetin" every night. I was treated just like another Mormon. Every Mormon house has large storeroom in the basement with a year's supply of food and water. They carefully cycle the food using the oldest first. John showed me around BYU's Design School. As a design exercise, the students had just completed a full-sized model (plug) of a car having only flat surfaces. It was faceted like a jewel. I immediately wanted to build it, instead of the design we were working on. But there was a complication about BYU ownership.

When I brought the drawing to Worth, he quickly found small flaws in the dimensions; the loft at Trumpy's had been very exacting! Worth and I began building the plug. The drawings showed a cross-sectional profiles every six inches. We made cardboard cut-outs of every section. We glued these to medium-density polyurethane panels, cut them out, and glued them together, forming a ridged model(plug). A lot of meticulous sanding was required to finalize the shape. Big car builders do this with modeling clay, which is very expensive. At this point, the body, doors, and hatches have to be coated in fiberglass. These parts are the "male". "Female" fiberglass molds are made from these.

Unfortunately, at this point Worth signed a contract to go to Costa Rica for a year, on some big fiberglass job. So it was up to me to finish the plug, build the molds, and build the prototype. I knew nothing about fiberglass. A wiser man would have sold the plug and ran for his life. Edwards rented a shop on Springhill Road at Tyson's Corners from Bill Scott Racing. Vicki worked five days a week at Varig Airlines. I worked Monday through Wednesday as a Position Classifier or Management Analyst at myriad Federal agencies. Thursdays through Sundays I worked at the Shop; Vicki worked with me on weekends. She became a better "fiberglasser" than I. I was to learn she can do anything; she's also a gourmet Chef. Being Lewis Carroll nuts, we named the car "The March Hare".

Bill Scott's building became overcrowded, so we moved down Springhill Road to a new facility being built by Del Ankers. Del Ankers's family owned the farmland that later became Tyson's Corner. He owned a photography shop on Capitol hill. He was also a White House photographer. Harry Truman would often end press meetings with: "Did you get that, Del?" To which Del would reply: "Yes sir, Mr. President". Del was a prince of a guy, I never heard anyone say anything negative about him. He was a husky "man's man" type of guy--always friendly. It was a huge building, but Del did all the maintenance work. When I went to UVA, there was a guy who went around downtown in bib-overalls, carrying a carpenters toolbox – he owned most of downtown Charlottesville. Del went around in a stoop, picking up screws, bolts, nails and other construction debris. The larger stuff he stored in his barn or yard at home, to the total dismay of his wife – Elizabeth.

Across the street from our shop, there was a classic car restoration shop. The principal car they were restoring was a 1930s Duesenberg Brougham, a one-off. They had disassembled it to the last bolt and were rebuilding it to original condition. They were doing it for Warren Beatty. His uncle, who looked like a clone, was supervising the job. One of the regular visitors was an elegant friendly gentleman named Robert Johnson. He would visit in priceless classic cars. The two jewels of his collection were a 1937 Mercedes-Benz 540K that had belonged to Fritz Thyssen – the German steel king. The other was a 1937 Delage-Delahaye D-8 120. Bob and his wife Carolyn drove new Mercedes. They lived in a scrumptious house, just across Chain Bridge Road from the Merrywood Estates – 1313 Merrie Ridge Road. Bob was a very friendly, the classic: "nice man". Vicki hadn't seen his cars; Carolyn showed us the Mercedes and Delage at their home.

It turned out, Bob had for years been running a large-scale operation dealing in containships of industrial wine, used primarily in salad dressing. He apparently held a virtual corner on the market. Over the years, a large number of elite investors, including many of the leading area banks had made a great deal of money by investing in the contracts. The rates of return were spectacular and many heavy-hitters begged to sign-up. It was a Ponzi Scheme. Somewhere around $60 million were lost.

A few weeks before the bubble burst, Bob had offered to sell me Thyssen's Mercedes for $35,000. He was trying to unload assets preparatory to a "hasty migration". I was sorely tempted to grab what was obviously "a steal". My attorney friend, Pat Echols, told me it was just as well that I didn't yield to temptation. All assets transferred in the last year were seized. Bob served four years in Allenwood Federal Prison, where he was know as "The Little Old Winemaker".

Bob was not the only big time Con Artiste I have known. Milton Addison was a Delta fraternity brother at W&M/VPI, now Old Dominion University. Milton and his brothers were well-known "Golden Glove" boxers in Norfolk. Aside from serving as a drinking associate at Delta parties, my only dealing with Milton was when Stan Pierce, Blair MacKenzie and I had helped him run a boxing tournament at the Norfolk Arena. The 1950s were the golden years of the "uranium craze". Milton and some associates had developed a miraculous "Uranium Upgrader". It was about 100 feet long, with large round rotating drums like concrete mixers, sporting myriad gears and levers, horns, bells and whistles. It sat by a runway in the middle of an Arizona desert. Planeloads of potential investors would be flown in. After a fiery speech by Milton, low-grade uranium ore would be shoveled into one end of the machine. The machine would go loudly into action: gears would turn, the giant drums would rotate, levers would crank, valves would blow-off steam, whistles would blow. Behold, out the other end would emerge golden cakes of high-grade uranium "yellow cake". Milton would mount the stage to deliver another fiery sermon. The "redeemed" multitudes would mob the stage to force Milton to accept their treasures. Eventually, the bubble burst and Milton ended up helping the state make license plates.

After the molds were finished we were going to need someone in the fiberglass manufacturing business to produce the bodies. I went to see T&P Plastics in Annapolis to see if they would be interested. T&P stood for Don Trumpy (John Trumpy's son) and Pat Patteson. They were building fiberglass cabin cruisers. They told me they used McClarin Plastics in Hanover, PA, because they could build the hulls cheaper than T&P could. Don Wine was the manager of McClarin. He was a big friendly guy, built like an NFL lineman: he wore "Lil Abner" boots. He was a Pennsylvania "Dutchman" who would have a drink with you. Hanover is an industrial town where a "Boilermaker" is the drink of choice. The slogan of March Hare was "Light as a feather; strong as a tank". The roof had a built-in roll-cage; steel tubing and balsa core. When factory visitors would question the Hare's strength, Don would kick the hell out of one the fenders with his "Lil Abner" boot, then say: "Let's go outside and do that to your car".

When Vicki and I finally finished the molds, we built a prototype. When I was growing up in the 1930's, if a man in the neighborhood had been building a far-out car, every kid in the area would have begged to help out. In the 1970's, the "Hippie Era", it was next to impossible to hire one. I lucked out one time with a great kid named Al Johnson. His father was the world famous Alvin"Tex" Johnson, Boeing's Chief Test Pilot. In a fly-by demonstration of the Dash 80, the Boeing 707 prototype, Tex barrel-rolled the plane twice. After that, every airline in the world wanted a 707.

Most of the March Hare buyers were engineers. One of them was Bruce Kirk; Project Manager of the Navy's Harpoon Program. He built a beautiful Porsche-powered one named "I'M QIK". He won a prize almost every time he entered it in a show. Unfortunately, not enough Bruce Kirks out there signed up. I designed a new advanced model named ECCO for Edwards Car Company. I almost finished building the full-scaled model – the Plug. But we were hemorrhaging money and it was breaking Vicki's heart. We finally threw in the towel – Exit March Hare!

March Hare Plug

March Hare

Victalina Maria Wells Thompson

Marilda Adams invited me to a Brazilian Christmas party at which everyone was dancing the Samba. Across the room a gorgeous girl was staring at me, I stared back. Then she walked across the room and stood face to face. She said: "You want Samba?" I said: "I don't know how". She said: "I teach". The next morning I called Marilda at the Embassy to get the CV of this lovely Brasileira. She was Vicki Thompson, she was working for her uncle Zeuxis Ferreira Neves, who was the Embassy representative of the Banco Nacional do Desenvolvimento Economico – BNDE. She lived with Rachel Wahl, the Social Secretary of the Embassy. The next night I took her to the Showboat to hear Charlie Byrd. We drank a gang of Martinis and fell in love. Three months later, March 17, 1961, St. Patrick's Day, we got married. Zeuxis and Rachel arranged a lovely reception at the Brasilian Embassy. Jackie Kennedy's dressmaker, Frankie Welsh, made Vicki's dress and attended the reception. The wedding, reception and everything were rushed because Zeuxis had arranged for Vicki and I to fly to Rio on maiden flight of Varig's first DC-8. We flew to Miami to meet the plane. We stayed at an Art Deco hotel in South Beach. I bought Vicki a yellow polka-dot bikini; a lot of people in South Beach noticed. Vicki looked like Miss Brasil!

Vicki and I and a couple of the pilot's wives were the only passengers. The plane was packed to the gunwales with spare parts and engines. Everything went as smooth as silk until we got to Dutch Guiana, where the plane developed an electrical problem. At about 3 o'clock in the morning we were flying with all lights on at tree-top level over the jungle looking for a WWII emergency field. The "admin-building" was out of a 1920's movie. When we landed at Santos Dumont in the morning we were met by a media horde.

Zeuxis had booked the Penthouse at the Hotel Miramar for us; the best location on Copacabana Beach. The Penthouse has a wrap-around balcony; you can see everything. Seaward, all of Copacabana and the

Sugarloaf. Landward, you can see the largest "favela" in Rio, Morro da Babilonia; where they filmed "Black Orpheous".

We started our Rio safari by going to Colombo's the world's most elegant cafe. This "belle epoque" masterpiece is an "art-nouveau" crystal palace. Mirrows from Belgium, stained glass from France, tiles from Portugal. The food is primarily "salgadinhos" (snacks) and pastries. The atmosphere is 19th Century. In a small bar between Copa and Ipanema, I tried my first "Caipirinha" Brasil's national drink. I loved it; we had a second. A small "Bateria" (drum group) wandered in playing Carnaval Sambas. I bought them a round; they kept playing; the bar began to fill. Soon everyone was dancing the Samba and having a hell of a time. Vicki's sister, Betty, and her fiancée, Francisco Scalamandre, joined us at the Miramar. They were a fun couple, always laughing. After doing the beaches at Copa, Ipanema, and Leblon with us , they drove us to Sao Paulo, the city were Vicki's was born and her family lived.

During one of our trips to Brasil in the 1970s, we were invited by Caribe da Rocha to spend New Years at the Hotel Nacional in Rio. Caribe was Manager of the Nacional. Caribe, his wife Leda and daughter Carla were friends of ours. Leda was a well-known ballerina; she and Carla ran a Ballet School in Rio. The Nacional is on the beach in the Gavea area. It is an imposing glass and steel cylinder designed by Oscar Niemeyer. One day while we were soaking up the sun and Caipirinhas by the pool, I saw a little boy about four years old desperately thrashing in the water – he was drowning. I dove in and pulled him out. The maid who was "watching" him, remained stupidly oblivious through it all. I often wondered what became of him.

Carnaval officially begins at mid-night, New Years. The top floor of the Nacional was a giant ballroom with a huge stage at one end. We were at one of the head tables with Caribe, Leda, Carla and a host of friends. An enormous "Bateria" was literally making the hair on the back of everyones neck stand up. Beautiful girls from one of the "Escolas de Samba" dragged everyone onto the floor to Samba. The singers were the two most famous Carnaval singers in Rio – Marlene and Odilon! At mid-night everyone sings "Feliz Ano Novo" and gives everyone a big "abraco". I was told one of the people who gave me a big "abraco" was the Chief of the "Esquadron da Morte".

Speaking of drums, we have a Japanese-Brasilian friend in Ibiuna, Marcello, who runs a school that teaches Taiko drums to children aged 6 to 18. They are well-known in Brasil and Japan. The band usually numbers about 30. They practice in a classroom not much larger than the band. Vicki and I have attended practice sessions. Your hair stands on end and all your vital organs vibrate.

In the 70's Ruben Berta, President of Varig, Brazilian Airline, and Assis Chateaubriand , Brasilian media mogul had been in Europe on an art buying expedition for Brasilian art museums in Sao Paulo. They returned via Washington to arrange a loan for Varig with various international bank organizations. The meetings were being arranged by Zeuxis Neves, Vicki's uncle, representing BNDE. Vicki was working with the secretaries of Berta and Chateaubriand. At the end of the day, when all business had been taken care of, the secretaries took Vicki shopping at Garfinckels. They bought her a fabulous pink cocktail dress covered in tiny crystals. The Ambassador threw a big reception at the Embassy for Berta and Chateaubriand. The new Miss Brasil happened to be at the party. Unfortunately, she was a teenage ragamuffin compared to Vicki. Many people thought Vicki was Miss Brasil.

As a result of Vicki's job at Varig, we were frequently invited to parties at the OAS and the Military and Naval delegations, where we got to know two of the future presidents of Brasil: Artur da Costa e Silva and Emilio Garrastazu Medici. Vicki was the hostess of a luncheon sponsored by Brasilinvest, at which President Ford was the principal speaker.

Vicki-and I at Kennedy Inauguration

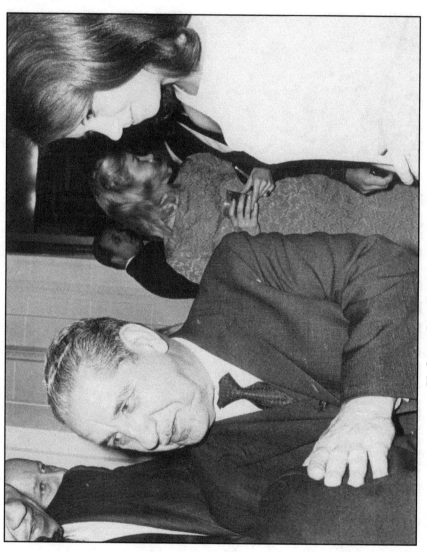

Vicki and Arthur da Costa e Silva

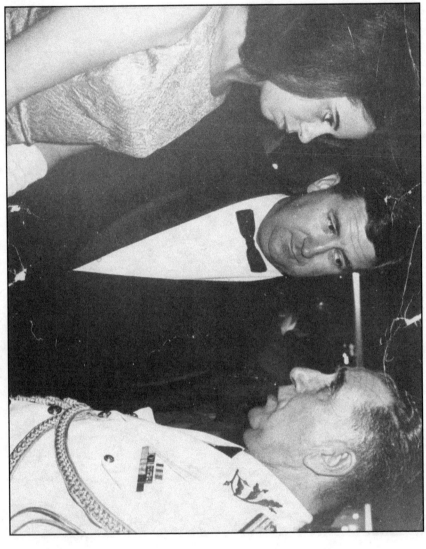

Vivki and I and Emilio Garrastazu Medici

Vicki and Ford

Hartwell Hooten Edwards
aka Eddie & Pug

Pug is my younger brother, named by me for his pugnacity. Like me, when he was in the Army, he was called Eddie, with him it stuck. Eddie Edwards could sell fleece-lined parkas in Hell. He has been very successful selling cars, boats, and real estate. In the 60s, 70s and 80s he managed multitudes of car agencies in the DC area. "Eddie Edwards" was legendary in the trade. Troubled agencies hired him as a "Messiah"; after he rescued their souls, he was cast into the outer-darkness. The car trade is a dirty business. When he moved South to Florida and Alabama, he went into boats and real estate. One day in Stuart, when I went to the Marina to pick him up for lunch Pug answered a wrong-number caller. She had never owned a boat, but in the next 20 minutes he sold her a 16-foot power-boat to get her started in boating. As we exited he said: "That'll pay for lunch".

Actually, like Jay Carsey, Pug should have been a politician. I visited him about three months after he moved to Gulf Shores, the "Redneck Riviera". At every bar, restaurant, gas station, bus stop, everybody knew him and called out his name. It was unbelievable. Every attribute of a "born politician" was second-nature to him. Differed gratification was an anathema to him and politics requires a long-range investment in time before the big payoffs start to roll in. It's a pity-- Pug would have been a "Duesy".

Pug's best friend was George Hoyer; they met in the first grade. George and Hood Roberts were the two funniest men I ever met. Like Hood, George was extremely bright. He scored the highest grades to that date on his American U entrance exams. George's humor was usually in the form of a running commentary on the ambient situation that would keep you hysterical. If you were well lubricated, you would be rendered helpless. Example:
Me: DC gangbangers are murdering with impunity.
George: Or anything else they can lay their hands on.

Eddie (left) in Korea (300 yards from "Joe Chink")

Joaquim Renato Correa Freire

Renato was my best friend in Brasil, we were like brothers, we drank and partied together. He was from a very old and prominent family. He knew anyone worth knowing in Brasil. He was an attorney, usually a principal in the firm. Renato was a great guy, always smiling, always solicitous: "A sua disposicao" as he would put it. I first met Renato in Dallas. He was taking a graduate law course at SMU; I was wholesaler for the Commonwealth Funds of San Francisco. Renato and Ana Maria had an apartment near the SMU campus; Vicki and I had an apartment near SMU. Vicki and Ana Maria met at Dallas airport, where they went to meet President Juscelino Kubitschek. Renato was a friend of the President; later at a reception for the President I met Renato. After the reception, the President invited the four of us to go to his hotel suite for drinks. That's how I met Renato and Ana Maria. We became good friends.

After we returned to Washington, I went to work for NASA, Vicki went to work for Varig Airlines. We became virtual commuters to Brasil (First-class, Beluga caviar, Dom Perignon). One of Renato's sisters, Marylu, was married to Homero Sousa e Silva, who was the partner of Walter Moreira Salles. They owned the largest bank in Brasil, ITAU, plus myriad other holdings like Mineracao Morro Velho SA, the largest gold mine in South America. Later they acquired Cia. Brasileira de Metalurgia & Mineracao (CBMM) which produces 85% of the world's Niobium; making them Brasil's richest family.

Niobium (Nb) is a rare earth metal, an alloying agent, used in the production of high strength, stainless, and heat resistant steels. They are critical in myriad industries: automotive, petrochemical, power generation, oil and gas pipelines, aircraft engines, particle accelerators, MRIs, etc.

On one of our trips to Rio, Homero's Citroen picked Renato and I up at Santos Dumont Airport and whisked us up to Homero and Marylu's palace in the hills. Incidently, the luxury Citroen back seats envelope you like a womb. The house was high in the hills overlooking most of Rio. The dining room reminded me of the one at Marjorie Post's Hillwood. The library was almost identical to Dieter Schmidt's, overstuffed leather chairs, walls paneled in Pau Brasil. There must be a standard Brasilian billionaire's library. Homero and Marylu had two children, Carlu and Christina. The Moreira Salles had four sons, Fernando, Pedro, Joao and Walter.

I spent a week or so with Renato and Ana Maria at their apartment on Praca Vila Boim. Renato's nephew, Carlu Sousa e Silva lived with them; Fernando Moreira Salles lived next door. I think Renato was supposed to be "keeping an eye" on them. They stayed pretty busy "entertaining" fabulous brasilieras.
Carlu was away, so I stayed in his room. One night, Renato asked Fernando to show me Sao Paulo's night life. We spent an "interesting" evening tooling around the downtown in his Porsche 911.

Later, Renato and Ana Maria broke up and Renato moved to Rio. He was now going with Kati, a Hungarian billionaire, whose family owned controlling interest in Portland Cement. Kati lived in a fantastic penthouse that over looked Ipanema Beach. Renato had a fantastic place high in the hills that overlooked much of Rio. It had a living room and balcony over 50 feet long, that looked down on the city. The high-vaulted ceiling had a long row of ceiling fans suspended by long pipes. The living room and balcony were used in the movie "Blame It On Rio". While I was visiting Renato, Kati gave a big party at her Ipanema penthouse. I remember two people from the party. One was a Frenchman Phillippe Le Blan, who owned France's largest department store. The other, John W. Mowinckel, who was on paper the Ministre-Counselor of the U.S. Embassy. Everyone said he was really the chief of the CIA team. Mowinckel was with Hemingway when they took over the Ritz bar on Paris's Liberation Day. While he was at work, Renato had his chauffeur take me down to the Rio de Janeiro Country Club on Ipanema Beach in the morning and pick me up there in the afternoon.

Renato married Kati and they lived for a while in a home by the ninth hole on the Gavea Golf Club. The fairways were lined with orchids.

I stayed at a little "pied-a-terre" in the garden. Most of the time you could walk around on and have the course to yourself. Later, Renato and Kati moved to a lovely home in Morumbi in Sao Paulo. They set up a law office for Renato primarily to handle Kati's complex legal affairs, due to the international nature of the Portland Cement business. Renato and I combed the bars and clubs in our continued guest for the "Perfect Martini". Renato often attempted to improve the end-product by instructing the bartenders to "somente mostre a garrafa" (only show the bottle) when adding the Vermouth. The bar in the Automobile Clube de Sao Paulo produced an excellent candidate. Also, the American Club at 95 Piccadilly, W.I, London made an outstanding "Martini". The San Fernando Club, about 30 kilometers outside Sao Paulo produced an excellent one; their "Wild Turkey" "Old Fashioned" was world class. The Clubhouse had a long balcony overlooking the fairway where squadrons of kaleidoscopic, polychromatic tropical birds flew perpetual patrols. Many of them were parrots, the Brasilians call them "Papagaios".

Renato knew everybody. He introduced me to Dom Pedro II's great grandson; pretender to the throne of Brasil. He was a very elegant, pleasant, and intelligent young man; he'd get my vote for King. When Renato told him I was married to a Brasilian, he pounded me on the back and said: "You're half Brasilian already". Another really interesting guy was Tony Almeida, his family owned Almeida Ferragens, the largest chain of hardware stores in Brasil. Tony was educated at Sandhurst and spoke with a British accent. He was blessed with a beautiful and sweet wife named Nana. His political views were somewhere to the right of Genghus Khan. He didn't like the hardware business, so he went in business leading safaris into the Amazon to hunt Jaguars.

Renato and Kati broke up over Renato's drinking. He briefly married a beautiful woman who looked like my wife Vicki, whom I was separated from at the time. I met her in DC when they were passing through; they had a very unpleasant divorce. Renato began partying it up; a lot of the time with Fernando. Two of Brasil's most eligible bachelors. Unfortunately, Renato's heart gave out and he died a young man. He was a splendid fellow; like a brother. He was always laughing. When you were with Renato you always felt like you were at a party. It was one of the great pleasures of my life to have known him. Saudades amigo!

Percy Putz

Another old and dear Brasilian friend is Percy Putz. Percy owns Elastic Plas, the largest rubber manufacturing plant in Brasil. Conveniently, he owns the largest rubber plantation in South America. His father was a German diplomat posted to Brasil in the 1930s, who split with the Nazis. He was a large, imposing, congenial man. Percy is an excellent businessman and a boon companion. His lovely wife, Sissa, is delightful. She smokes long slim cigarettes, whose "paper" are corn husks; they're different and delicious. One of our favorite dining spots was the Terraco on Isla Porchat. It is located high on Porchat's hill that overlooks all of Santos's fabulous beach. There are few more spectacular vistas in the world.

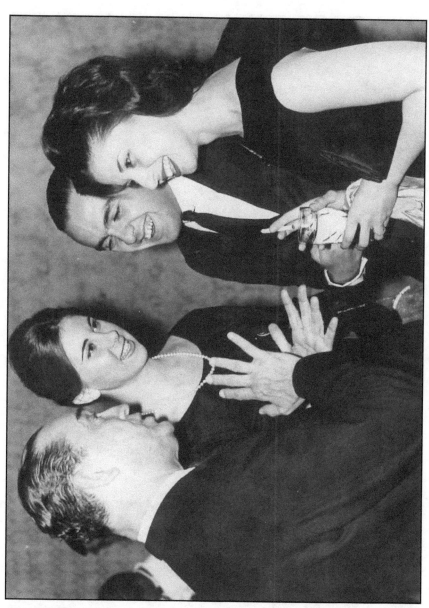

Kubitschek, Vicki, Renato, AnaMaria

Kubitschek, Vicki, Edwards, AnaMaria

Hans Dieter Schmidt

Dieter's father, Albano, established Fundicao TUPY S.A. in 1936. Upon his death in 1958, Dieter became president at age 26. Under Dieter's command, TUPY became the largest foundry in South America. Dieter had grown up in the same block with Vicki's cousin Clovis Thompson de Carvalho, they were best friends. Dieter married Maria Claudia Quintanilha, from one of the oldest families in Brasil; they had three sons, Albano, Rodrigo and Fernando. They had a home in Sao Paulo, but their principal home was in Joinville not far from the factory. TUPY was having the annual meeting of the Board of Directors. Clovis was on the Board, Vicki and I were invited to fly to Joinville with Clovis and spend a few days at Dieter's home.

The home was designed by Oscar Niemeyer; designer of Brasilia. It occupied the top of a private mountain that overlooked Joinville. It was enormous. The portico seemed almost as large as that of the White House. Everything was white marble. At the far end of the hotel lobby scale grand foyer was a magnificent grand staircase that swept in a great arc to the upper floor bedroom suites. Aside from the master suite, there was one for each son, plus guest suites. German Chancellor Helmut Schmidt was a frequent guest. Dieter put us in Schmidt's apartment. It was lush, everything done in deep burgundy Pau Brasil (Brasilwood); the bathroom in a beautiful marble.

Dieter and Maria Claudia's bedroom was across the hall. The Romanesque bathroom was enormous, with a fountained walk-in tub; everything in fabulous marble.

A galaxy of rooms radiated from the grand foyer: living room, dining room, billiards, library, breakfast, TV lounge. The library was almost identical to that of the Sousa e Silva's in Rio; standard Brasilian billionaire. Most rooms had floor to ceiling windows overlooking the garden. Several opened on patios with ponds, statuary, and flower beds. The house stood in the middle of acres of garden. Paths wandered among every kind of tree, scrub, and flower that grew in Brasil. The paths overlooked Joinville and the surrounding countryside. Scattered around the garden were a swimming pool, tennis courts, and a pitch and put course. An enormous Niemeyer sculpture about the size of the average suburban house was structured of huge domino-like granite tiles covered in indescipherable hieroglyhics.

Our second day we visited Fundicao TUPY. It was huge. We watched them cranking-out masses of engine blocks. All the supervisors with clipboard were blond blue-eyed supermen. You had to be careful; everywhere there were large containers of harmless looking parts that would burn your hand off if you picked one up – they were white-hot. Dieter was especially proud of their big trade-school; all the workers took classes in German.

Most rich Brazilians had Mercedes; Dieter thought they attracted attention; he had a Ford Galaxie. The next day Dieter turned over the Galaxie and his chauffeur to us for a tour of the State of Santa Catarina and Blumenau. The population of Santa Catarina is primarily of German or Italian descent. The homes of the masses are usually small, well built, colorful, and immaculate. The state is neat, clean, and beautiful. Our driver, Karl, of German stock, was very pleasant, and really knew the countryside. We had lunch at a German restaurant in the country that looked like the one in Cabaret. Blumenau looks like it was transplanted from Bavaria. The town was filled with arts and crafts shops, primarily glassware.

Dieter was a splendid man. Rich, powerful, intelligent, but "plain as an old shoe". Very laid back with a great sense of humor; you couldn't help but like him. Dieter was very active politically. Many saw him as the future Governor of Santa Catarina or President of Brasil. In 1981, while serving as Secretario do Estado da Industria de Santa Catarina, Dieter and his cabinet were all killed when their plane crashed into a mountain in a storm. Another splendid man chopped down in the prime of life. It was a tragic loss for his family, his friends, and for Brasil.

Dieters Portico

Clovis,Edwards,Dieter

Robert Taylor Taylor III (RT) / Peter M. Adams

A high percentage of UVA students used to go to Lynchburg in the summer to meet the two year language requirement. Lynchburg College conducted high intensity courses in Spanish, French and German. That's where I met RT Taylor and Pete Adams, who became lifetime friends. Pete Adams was a direct descendant the "1776" John Adams. Both were History majors at UVA during the 1946-50 "GI Bill" period when the universities were inundated with the "The Greatest Generation". Pete had been in the "Mighty 8th Air Force". He was a B-17 waist-gunner shot down on his 15th mission and imprisoned in "Stalag 17". RT was a Heavy Construction Engineer in New Guinea and Luzon; he saw action in the Philippines and Okinawa. I was a Combat Engineer in Patton's Third Army.

Pete had been educated at the best Ivy League prep schools; UVA was a breeze. After graduation he taught for a while at the prestigious Miller School near Charlottesville. RT also went into teaching in Raleigh, NC. Over the years, RT and I sought out good "watering-holes" in divers places. Greensheild's in Raleigh was a mini-brewery: wheat/oatmeal stouts, high wing-back leather chairs, roaring fireplace, good food cheap, beautiful and attentive "serving wenches". Near Greensheilds was the best breakfast restaurant on the planet -- "Big Ed's". It was a big old open barny place. A typical $5 platter had two eggs, bacon, sausage, scraple, grits or hash browns, biscuit and coffee. The pancakes were the size of dinner plates.

RT is an outdoorsman. The Appalachian Trail is overrun with wildlife: deer, bear, wild turkey and rattlesnakes. I've never seen so many rattlesnakes. One summer day , RT, Ellen (his wife) and I were hiking the trail to Big Flat Mountain. We stopped to admire a huge Crabapple tree, loaded with a zillion apples. As we started to go, a sixth sense told me to look down. Just where my next step would have taken me stood the biggest rattlesnake I've ever seen. Coiled, head erect at about 15 inches, mouth open, fangs bared. We broke the Olympic record for the "backward leap". Now he shook his huge rattle; he had been waiting as silent as the grave.

Pete's mother, Evelyn Moore Adams (Red) was a well-known ghost-writer for Capital Hill heavy-hitters; few politicos write their own stuff. Red's parties were a who's who of the hill. After the parties Pete and Marilda (Pete's wife) always bought home a carload of leftovers. Marilda's father was a Brasilian army General, Arcy da Rocha Nobrega, a good friend of Presidente Getulio Vargas.

Cecil Mesic/Stan Pearce

Cecil, Stan, and I met at Ruffner Junior High School in 1937. We went from there to Granby High. We belonged to the same Boy Scout Troop – Troop 49. Cecil was Junior Assistant Scout Master; Stan and I were Patrol Leaders. There were a lot of good camping sites in the Norfolk/Virginia Beach area, usually near a beach. Troop 49 had Army war surplus pyridimal tents; one for each patrol and one for the Scoutmaster, Assistant Scoutmaster, and Junior Assistant. Campouts were great fun: hiking, fishing, swimming, arts and crafts, merit-badge tests, and lots of campfire time singing songs like "Abdul Abulbul Amir".

Cecil and I used to camp in the Azalea Gardens which adjoined Norfolk Airport. The whole area was covered in 100 foot tall long leaf pine; the ground underneath blanketed in pine needles six inches deep, which created an excellent mattress . We pitched our tent by one of the lakes, so we could fish and shoot Cottonmouth Water Moccasins. Cottonmouth are venomous, territorial, and aggressive. You have to be a pretty good shot to get them, because only their head sticks out of the water as they swim by 20 or 30 feet away. In that era, teenage boys commonly went around with .22 rifles or hunting bows, you could hunt and shoot almost everywhere. Today's teenagers have been brainwashed, sheltered, and controlled all their lives by the government. If given guns, they would probably wipe each other out in a week. You have to be accustomed to guns; I got my .22 when I was twelve.

Stan and Cecil were special: strong, tough, good, easy-going guys, always with a hardy laugh and a big smile. Cecil introduced me to classical and semi-classical music. The three of us used to hike around at night singing operetta music like "Stout Hearted Mens" and "We are the Musketeers". One night we hiked to a Carnival ground across town where I saw my first naked woman -- "for just 25 cents more, she takes off absolutely everything!" Cecil dropped out of Granby in 1942 to join the Marine Corps; he fought in the South Pacific. Stan and I went in the Army in 1943; he went to the Pacific; I went to Europe. Stan won the Soldiers Medal for saving a guy from drowning during an invasion. Cecil got married and started a family during the war. After the war, he went to work for Newport News Shipbuilding Co and retired from there. Stan and I went to W&M/VPI for two years; from there he went to Miami U in Ohio, I went to UVA. At W&M/VPI we belonged to Delta, the principle drinking fraternity. I met a couple of lifetime friends in Delta: Blair MacKenzie and Frank Hallowell. Frank played trumpet in the College band, Tommy Newsome played trombone. Tommy later played in Johnny Carson's Tonight Show Band; he arranged the music; he was in Delta.

Stan's family were very poor during the "Great Depression". At Miami U, he met and married Abbie whose family was wealthy. He ran a large tile operation in Tampa/St. Pete. Abbie inherited the family money and Stan retired. The poor boy from Fairmount Park now played golf and drove a Porsche 911. Stan dropped dead under a shade tree on the golf course. He was probably laughing. Cecil always looked like a body-builder; he still did in his seventies. He died peacefully in his sleep – the nicest guy I ever knew!

George William Whitehurst

Bill was born in Norfolk, Virginia on March 12, 1925. He graduated from Maury High School in 1942. He served in the Pacific Theater from 1943 to 1946, as a radioman/gunner on a Grumman TBF Avenger Torpedo Bomber. When his machine gun jammed while strafing a Jap airfield, Bill blasted away with his .38 Smith&Wesson. He was part of the big fly-over of the Battleship Missouri at the Jap surrender; 1200 carrier planes and 300 B-29s. He received his B.A. From Washington and Lee in 1950; his M.A. from UVA in 1951; his Ph.D. From West Virginia U in 1952. He began his collegiate teaching career in 1953 at the Norfolk Division of the College of William and Mary (V.P.I.) known to everyone as "The Division". It became Old Dominion College in 1962. He taught European history and had his own news analyst program at WTAR-TV. This exposure led him into politics. In 1968, he was elected to the U.S. House of Representatives, where he served from January 3, 1969 to January 3, 1987. He served on the Armed Services Committee, the Select Committee on Intelligence, and on the Ethics Committee. When he retired from the House, Bill returned to Old Dominion University as the Kaufman Lecturer in Public Affairs.

I met Bill at UVA, but didn't get to know him until after graduation back in Norfolk. He was a friend of my good buddy, R.T. Taylor. Bill had invited RT and I to his classroom at the Division to see "Triumph of the Will". Bill used it in his Modern European History Course. It was Leni Riefenstahl's famous film of the 1934 Nazi Party Rally in Nurnberg . Staged by Albert Speer in the gigantic Zeppelin Stadium, tens of thousands of SS, SA, and Hitler Youth marched to the beat of massed bands and drums. Thousands of Hitler Youth pounded thousands of drums, screaming Seig Heil, Seig Heil, Seig Heil (Hail Victory) at the top of their lungs. When the crescendos reached fever pitch, and his students were keeping step with their feet, Whitehurst would flip-on the lights and say: "Now, do you see what happened?".

The government had stored tons of Nazis art and documents in the Torpedo Factory in Alexandria. Members of Congress could borrow the art to decorate their offices. Bill had a full-sized statue of a Hitler Youth and two of the most famous German World War II war paintings. One was "Russian Roads", a 1943 painting of a column of German infantry plodding along a muddy, rutted road in a storm. The other was of German Combat Engineers (Pioneeren) making a river assault. The German government gave Bill "Russian Roads", which hung in his Norfolk home along with eight Herman Herzogs. Herzog was German-American landscape artist, who lived between 1831 and 1931. The Whitehurst's waterfront condo looked down on the long erotic bow of BB-52 New Jersey berthed outside their window. Bill later gave "Russian Roads" back to the German government, they awarded him a medal.

Occasionally, Bill would invite me for the "Bean Soup" at the House Dining Room, where we usually discussed weapon systems. Sometime, Vicki and I would join Jeanie and Bill for dinner at someplace like the Capital Hill Club. One Sunday afternoon, Vicki invited three of the books protagonists (Butz, Carsey, Whitehurst) to a Brasilian "feijoada' at our home. We wanted them to get better acquainted; they had a lot in common – intelligence work, weapon systems. Jay and Nancy had just returned from Russia, and Jay was telling about something that happened at the Bolshoi. Nancy suddenly blurted out: "Oh shut up, Jay. I'll tell it. You always mess up everything". Jay made his famous exit shortly after that.

Lewey Gilstrap

Lew is one of nature's noblemen. Like the cavalry he always stands ready to ride to your rescue. About twice a year he rescues me from some computer disaster. He keeps up to speed on everything. As with Gillespie, when we get together, I always open with: "Well, Lew, what's new?" Then, I relax and enjoy a lecture on some new tech development.

Lew is a renaissance man. As a child, he taught himself music. He plays a number of musical instruments: piano, clarinet, sax, flute, etc. He taught himself music theory. He transposes at sight. He was a union musician at age 15, playing in bands like Dick Jones and his commanders. In WWII he played in the First Army Hdqrs band at Ft. Jay on Governor's Island, NY.

CURRICULUM VITA

Lewey Gilstrap has a BS degree in Engineering Physics from the Universityf Oklahoma. He did extensive graduate work in Physics, Mathematics, Electrical Engineering and Mechanical Engineering. Lew's professional career included more than 40 years in the fields of Artificial Intelligence and Adaptive Systems. He was one of the Founders of Adaptronics, Inc. in 1961, serving as Executive Vice President until 1971, when he left to become a freelance consultant in the field. While at Adaptronics, he co-designed the first industrial grade artificial neural network, which was used in many applications. His team also was the first to apply artificial neural networks to the evaluation of experimental psychotropic drugs using all-night EEG sleep records as input data. During his career, he also taught a variety of technology courses at several Colleges, including more than 5 years teaching information technology courses to graduate students at the Johns Hopkins University. His professional society contributions included serving as Secretary, then Vice President for programs, for the American Society for Cybernetics. He is currently writing a book on Robotics.

Carl H. Middleton

About twice a month, Carl and I have lunch at The Washington Golf and Tennis Club at a table overlooking the 18th hole. I usually get things started with: "Well, Carl, what's new?" This is followed by about two hours of first-rate "cabbages and kings" conversation. We talk about everything under the sun and are usually in total agreement. We have become boon companions – Kipling's "trusty chums". Carl is author of "Great Thoughts: A Conservative's History of Western Civilization", a 1200 plus page selection of the Conservative Book Club. The book is a one volume education and addictive. Carl has a lovely wife, Colin, and three sons.

Two Purposes of *Great Thoughts*

Great Thoughts is a new book concept. Half is quotations of the West's preeminent thinkers and movers and half is a history of Western civilization that places the authors' words within the context of their times. It features both the noblest and the most destructive men and women to extract lessons from the past. History and literature help us to understand how humans act, which allows us to become more prudent in our judgments about individuals and groups. And as C. S. Lewis said, "You are what you read."

Great Thoughts also seeks to preserve the West's rare and precious precepts that gave birth in 1776 to a free republic admist a sea of despots ruling destitute peoples. As Lawrence W. Reed wrote, "Our hope is that through education men and women will understand the moral, philosophic, and economic principles that undergird a free society; that they will appreciate the direct connection between those principles and their material and spiritual welfare."

Mea Culpa, Mea Culpa, Mea Maxima Culpa

Great Thoughts lacks a scholar's refinements because it was compiled by a "man in the arena"—a U.S. Marine officer, lawyer, and businessman. Surveying 3,500 years of Western civilization has undoubtedly led to errors in fact and opinion, but hopefully it gets right the inflection points in Western civilization. It includes wonderful quotations without citations because the authoritative liberal anthologies omit many great conservative quotations. I lacked platoons of scholars and decades of time to track down the citations. Also, its commentaries warrant volumes of footnotes, but the virtue of surveys is brevity. Its bias is conservative, which George Will defined as "realism about human nature and government's competence."

Three Special Features

Most quotation anthologies ignore economics and business principles. *Great Thoughts* emphasizes neoclassical economic theories (especially Austrian) because utopian Marxist and Keynesian theories poisoned Western politics. Second, it contains insights from over 60 business executives and professional investors. Third, *Great Thoughts* is chock full of lively anecdotes, ironic humor, and astonishing historical asides "too good to check out." William F. Buckley Jr. said of a draft of the book, it "is full of sparkle."

Author Biography

Carl H. Middleton was born in 1938 and raised in Tuscumbia, Alabama. He received a B. A. from Princeton University (Woodrow Wilson School of Public and International Affairs) and a L.L.B. from the University of Virginia Law School. He served as a captain in the U. S. Marine Corps, practiced law, was president of a secondary lead smelting company, and spent 20 years in international business, the last ten years as the Washington representative of a subsidiary of the London Economist Group. He has made presentations on "Business Strategies for the Global Economy" in the U.S., Europe, China, and Japan. He lives in Arlington, Virginia, is married, and has three sons.

St. Goar/Sankt Goar

I was in the 243rd Engineer Combat Battalion, Company B, second platoon, second squad. The 243rd was assigned to Patton's Third Army on 12/23/44. Our platoon was occupied with the myriad chores of engineers: building roads and bridges, clearing mine fields. On 1/17/45, our squads 2 ½ ton truck ran over a German AT mine; four guys were wounded. On 1/25/45 Sgt Bates and I were operating mine detectors in minefield near Rament. The minefield was covered in deep snow and infested with AP mines. Bates stepped on a wooden Shuh mine and got a very bad leg wound. We all liked Bates. The grandmother whose house we were billeted in dug up a bottle of five star Calvados from the keller; we drank a toast to Bates.

In February 1945, in the middle of the Battle of the Bulge, Johnny Barlow, Johnny Glushek and I got a three-day pass to Nice. We flew over the Alps in a C-46 to the airport in Nice. We stayed in a small hotel near the Ruhl Hotel and the Casino, which was now a USO. We went to the Chanel factory in Grasse; the Opera in Old Nice; sang in the chorus of an Oklahoma road company; went to dance every night at the Casino; the piano bar at the Ruhl.

On March 25th, the 243rd was assigned to support the 89th Infantry Division in their assault on the Rhein at Sankt Goar. Company B was assigned to build the Floating Steel Treadway Bridge. At Sankt Goar the Rhine is 250 meters wide; the Rhine Gorge; the swiftest point in the river. The site of the legendary Lorelei! St. Goar lies in the middle of the gorge; Koblenz is 24 km north; Bingen is 25 km southeast. Above St. Goar stand the ruins of Burg Rheinfels, the largest and most famous castle on the Rhein. Across the river lies the sister town of St. Goarhausen, with its own castles, Katz and Maus (Cat and Mouse). There lived the river barons, who from their castles on the hills, exacted tribute from passing ships. The famous Lorelei is just up stream on the St. Goarhausen side. Lorelei was a huge rock formation from which the golden-haired maidens of Heine's poem lured unwary sailors to untimely deaths on the shoals below. Napoleon's forces occupied St. Goar between 1794 and 1813. During this period, parts of Burg Rheinfels were blown up.

In typical fashion, Montgomery assembled a gigantic force for his Rhine assault in the Ruhr area. He amassed hordes of tanks and artillery, a Navy of landing craft, plus airborne divisions to drop behind the German lines, backed by an air force that would blacken the skies. In a polar opposite strategy, Patton planned for the Third Army to take the Rhine "on the run" with no advance preparation. He selected the Rhine gorge, the swiftest part of the river. This stretch of the river was the worst possible place for an assault crossing. Patton selected it in the belief that "the impossible place is usually the least well defended". Not quite!

At St Goar, the 168th Combat Engineers were to ferry the 89th Division infantry across the river in small unpowered assault boats. These were small wooden boats powered by four engineers with paddles, usually carrying about ten huddled infantrymen. At 0200, the first boats shoved off. They were hit by German 88mm guns in St Goarhausen before they could get away from the shore. When what was left of the 31 assault boats got about a third of the way across, the Germans hosed them down with quad 20mm antiaircraft guns – called "Flakwagens". The "Flakwagens" ignited a gasoline barge the Germans had mounted in midstream. By the light of inferno, those on shore watched boats exploding "in a geyser of flying wood and sprawling bodies". Some of the engineers and infantry had managed to get across; during the night small-arms fire could be heard in St. Goarhausen. Another crossing at wooded area downstream from St Goar was met by "Flakwagens". At Oberwesel, engineer-manned DUKWs, LCVP, and LCM were used for the crossing. These were supported by tanks and self-propelled guns lining the waterfront. Oberwesel became the main crossing site; by evening St. Goarhausen had been cleared by troops from Oberwesel.

B Company of the 243rd started work on March 26th. They started by installing an anchor cable. A one-inch cable was dragged across the river by a half-inch cable that had been towed across the river by powerboat. On the St Goarhausen side the cable was anchored to a large tree. An

"A" frame was used to elevate the cable out of the water. On the St. Goar side, a deadman was built out of two logs 15 feet long and 12 inches in diameter. A small stone building served as the "A" frame. They tried to use powerboats to tow the pontons to the end of the bridge; it didn't work. The river was so swift the boats kept getting swept under the bridge. They decided the pontons had to be towed out by hand. Two men were designated for this job – Fred Pease and I. Fred and I didn't have any trouble, but you had to shout at each other to be heard.

At any given time, one squad of the second platoon was on the bridge. Generally, the operation went off without a hitch. One problem, the Germans kept sending SS swimmers with satchel charges to try to blow up the bridge. We stationed guys with M-1s and flashlights along the bridge. The SS guys were only wearing swimming trunks and carrying satchel charges. The water was ice-cold. We pulled several of the half-frozen and helpless guys out of the river and sent them ashore with our medic, Joe Bitsko. The squads took turns on the bridge. On one of our breaks during the night, our squad climbed the hill to Burg Rheinfels. We found a promontory cliff sticking out of the ruins that provided a box seat to the action on the river. When I went back to St. Goar in the 80s, Burg Rheinfels had been converted to a posh hotel. The restaurant had a semi-circular balcony built directly above the promontory we had stood on that night. During the night, someone discovered a Wehrmacht warehouse full of Rhein wine, which was spread rapidly through the Company. Some resourceful pioneer loaded every truck in the Battalion. Major Howard Moreland, Battalion Exec, showed up at the bridgehead, loaded with St Goar's best, and had to be fished out of the river. Everything went glowingly until the next day. The Wehrmacht began lobbing some heavy stuff into the river trying to take out the bridge. They obviously had some forward observers in St Goar or St Goarhausen, because their aim kept improving. Discretion being the better part of valor; it was decided to evacuate the bridge until things improved. Everybody took cover in town. Pease and I hunkered down behind a wall next to a waterfront hotel – Hotel Zum Goldenen Lowen. When the shelling began to taper-off, Pease nudged me and said: "Eddie, I'll race you to the bridge!" I said: "Let's go!" With an occasional shell falling and the Battalion watching, Pease and I raced to the bridge and began towing a ponton. We beckoned for everyone to join us. Newsreel cameramen in a powerboat filmed the whole thing. My mother and brother saw us in the newsreels. With no more excitement; we finished the bridge that afternoon and went back to the bivouac area.

A footnote on St. Goar. The two most famous pictures of all the Rhine crossings were taken at St. Goar. The first shows the GI's of the 168th Combat Engineers and the 89th Division huddled in an assault boat. That picture is used on the cover of The Guns at Last Light by Rick Atkinson. The other picture is of our guys putting together a steel treadway ponton on the shore. The only guy in the picture without a helmet is my best buddy, Johnny Glushek, wielding a sledgehammer. Johnny was our hammer man. He was from South Philly, like Rocky. He was a great guy; always crooning some Sinatra song. The man sitting on the treadway, facing the camera is Colonel Otis Skinner, the Battalion CO. A couple of weeks before the crossing, I had hopped over a tree with an axe in my hand and cut a deep gash in my knee. The doctor patched it up with a butterfly bandage. When Pease and I raced to the bridge it got ripped open. A couple of days later I had a golf ball size swollen lymph gland in my crotch. They sent me to the rear to get sewn up. The ambulance was filled with GIs and one big blond SS trooper. The SS guy's arm was all shot up and a couple of GIs were trying to pull his SS ring off the finger of his shot-up arm. He was grimacing in pain, so I barked-out: "Leave the guy alone, can't you see you're hurting him?" Whereupon, the SS man turned to me and said in perfect English: "Thank you sir, you are a gentleman".

At the end of the war our platoon was sent to Zwickau to run a Yugoslav POW camp housed in a Wehrmacht Kaserne in the middle of town. We were billeted in the mansion of the ex-manager of the Auto Union factories. Before the war, the factories had produced the Horch and Audi; during the war, they produced Staff Cars and Half-Tracks. The place was a palace; huge crystal chandeliers, marble floors; each of us had a large private room. The Kaserne housed thousands of Yugoslav partisans, about evenly divided between followers of Tito and Mihailovitch; it was a powder-keg! During the day, they were being processed and sent home. At night, they threw wild parties in the large drill hall. One of our squads manned the gatehouse (vor dem grossen Tor) sort of like graphite control rods to prevent a runaway reaction. One night, it all erupted with screams of: "Zivia Tito", "Zivia Mihailovitch"; guys dueling with swords. We walked into the melee, fired our M-1s into the ceiling and ended the Opera! Soon after, the Russians took over; it was their zone. During the Russian occupation, the old Auto Union plant produced Trabants.

Later, our platoon ran a camp of Hungarian Army POWs near Straubing. They were repairing a bridge over the Danube. Every Hungarian is a musician; when transporting them to work, they were playing an orchestra of instruments. Their CO was an elegant man who looked like Vittorio De Sica. Some days he would come to our barracks and in flawless English ask to borrow a couple of rifles, so his men could supplement their rations. The woods were filled with German deer about the size of Yellow Labs. Later, his staff would bring over platters of grilled venison steaks.

On December 14, 1994, the King and Queen of Belgium, Albert II and Paola, hosted a 50th Anniversary tribute to the Veterans of the Battle of the Bulge at the DAR Hall. The Symphonic Band of the Belgian Guides Regiment provided the music. At the reception, the Royal couple thanked each soldier individually and gave him a picture autographed: "Thank you. We will never forget." I sat next to General J. Lawton Collins, Jr. and his wife. They ran a vineyard in Middleburg and were very pleasant. His father, General "Lightning Joe" Collins was commander of the VII Corps in the Battle of the Bulge. The Battle of the Bulge was the largest battle fought by the U. S. Army in World War II.

St. Goar - Glushek (without helmet)

Men on bridge near shore - Edwards and Pease

Glushek, Olanoff, Edwards and Barlow

GIs

"Imagine this. In the spring of 1945, around the world, the sight of a twelve-man squad of teenage boys, armed and in uniform, brought terror to people's hearts. Whether it was a Red Army squad in Berlin, or a German squad in Holland, or a Japanese squad in Manila, that squad meant rape, pillage, looting, wanton destruction, senseless killing. But there was an exception: a squad of GIs. A sight that brought the biggest smiles you ever saw to people's lips, and joy to their hearts."

"Around the world this was true, even in Germany, even – after September 1945 – in Japan. This was because GIs meant candy, cigarettes, C-rations, and freedom. America had sent the best of her young men around the world, not to conquer but to liberate, not to terrorize but to help. This was a great moment in our history."

The Victors by Stephen E. Ambrose

Alpenstrasse/Tegernsee

Before you die, see the most beautiful region on Earth – the Alpenstrasse. It runs through the Bavarian Alps for about 280 miles; every mile is breathtaking. You are always passing through meadows and farms, bordered by Christmas tree toped hills and mountains. Every five kilometers you come upon a fairytale village that Disney only wishes he could copy. The Alpine houses are almost smothered in flowers. There are always fabulous hotels, inns, restaurants, and arts and crafts shops. Often the restaurants are famous for gourmet cuisine and are usually cheap to reasonable. The regional beer is wiessbeer /whitebeer/ wheatbeer. It's usually served in frost covered liters; it's delicious, strong, and cheap.

I always stayed on the Tegernsee which is a lake located near the center of the Alpenstrasse about 30 miles southeast of Munchen; it's approximately four miles long and one mile wide. Five towns line its shores: Tegernsee, Kreuth, Gmund , Bad Wiessee, and Rottach-Egern. Your choice of beautiful places to stay are legion. One of my favorites is the Angermaier in Rottach-Egern. It sits in the middle of a large orchard, looking across a great meadow to a mountain used by sailplanes and hang-gliders that land in the orchard. Inside and out, it's alpine-style is fabulous. The last time I checked, a double room with breakfast costs $50 per day. For something pricier and historical as hell, there's the Lederer am See in Bad Wiessee. This is where on the night of June 30, 1934, Hitler and the SS arrested Ernst Roehm and the top brass of the SA in the "night of the long knives". At that time it was called the Hanselbaur. It borders the lake, a large park, and a casino. The water of the lake is so pure that the paper for most of the world's money is made in Gmund. Bad Wiessee, Rottach-Egern, and Tegernsee are gems. Every Sunday, half of Bavaria seems to go to the Park Hotel Resi von der Post in Bad Wiessee; the specialty is fresh fish from the lake. The parking lot is packed with Audis, BMWs and Mercedes. One Sunday, a 1937 Tatra, that looked brand new was parked there. The owner not only showed me all the bells and whistles; he let me drive it! This was the car Porsche modeled the VW after. Another place everybody goes is huge bier hall bordering a park in Tegernsee, the Braustuber where platters of white radish come with the bier. Just outside Rottach-Egern, you can take a fast cable car up the Wallberg Mountain for a spectacular view of the whole Tegernsee area, while dining at the Panorama. At the foot of the cable car lift there is a beautiful alpine restaurant with a large scenic balcony – the Alpinwildpark. You sit on the balcony with a frosty liter of wiessbier and watch the deer. When you get back in Rottach-Egern go the Seehotel Uberfahrt for a 3-star Michelin meal.

There are story book villages like Schliersee and Bayrischzell that are only 20 to 30 kilometers from Tegernsee. Or it is an easy one day trip to Neuschwanstein, Herrenchiemsee, Linderhof, Mittenwald, Oberammergau, and Salzburg. Herrenchiemsee was Ludwig II's attempt to copy Versailles. Oberammergau is filled with the best woodcarvers in the world. You can easily spend the day in one shop. Aside from religious objects like crucifixes and martels, they carve everything – furniture, mantels, toys, canes. It's expensive, but its the best. Nearly all buildings are covered with allegorical Luft Malerei frescoes. Many of the farm building in the area are a combination Inn and Barn. They are fun places to stay; the people on one end, the cows on the other. You hear mooing and cowbells in the AM and PM. Bad Wiessee, Rottach-Egern, and Tegarnsee have band and orchestra concerts in the park. Rottach-Egern has an annual Rosstagfest (Horse Festival) in which highly decorated animals, wagons, carts, and carriages parade with oampah bands; everyone dressed in Tracht (Bavarian costumes). The parade goes to a fair ground just outside town with bandstands and picnic tables for a lot of musik, bier trinken, essen, and Gamutlichkeit.

Mosel/Rhein

The Mosel from Bernkastel-Kues to Koblenz is the most beautiful part of the Mosel. It's about 60 kilometers as the crow flies, but it's as curvy as a snake. The Rhein from Koblenz to St.Goar is the most beautiful part of the river; it's about 30 kilometers. These sections of both rivers are flanked by vineyards and dotted with storybook castles. I found a lovely room in a Gasthaus in Kues with bath, balcony and breakfast for $25 per day. The breakfast was big enough to last all day; the bath was more modern than my own. Every room had a private parking space across the street. There was an Aldi's two blocks away. The Gasthaus owner was the ex-Police Chief of Kues.

The twin town, Bernkastel is just across the bridge from Kues; about 150 yards. The Mosel cruise boats dock along the quay in Bernkastel. My balcony looked directly across the Mosel at Burg Landshut; an ancient castle. The vineyard adjoining the Burg Landshut vineyard produces the best Mosel wine – Bernkastler Doctor – it is the most expensive piece of land in Germany. Bernkastel is another fairytale town; most building covered in allegorical frescoes and smothered in flowers. Bernkastel is filled with shops, restaurants, and bars, particularly wine bars. One sunny noon, I was having lunch and enjoying a band concert in the main square, when a group of well-dressed couples arrived. I was alone at a four-chair table, so in the German manner, one couple asked if they could join me. Which I answered in the German manner – Bitte. They were members of some elite wine lovers society touring the Mosel. The gentleman at my table was the retired Minister of Economics of Germany. He talked about Mosel; he told me about Bernkastler Doctor. After lunch, the group was going to cross the bridge to Kues. At the foot of the bridge was a Wine Museum, filled with antique vineyard equipment. Under the Wine Museum was a huge keller with a reserved section for every Mosel winery. You bought a wine glass in the Museum for DM17 and descended to the vast keller where you could try all the Moels, there were over 150 vineyards represented. Keller employees only opened the bottles; you served yourself. You could drink all day long. The Economics Minister and his wife invited me to join the group for the Keller visit, which I did. He even bought me the glass. I hadn't noticed the police presence at the Museum, but the next morning at breakfast, my Police Chief host asked me if I enjoyed my Museum visit.

Actually, this was not my first visit to the Mosel. In March 1945, my outfit was part of the Third Army dashing for the Rhine. On the towering walls of the vineyards lining the Mosel, the Germans had painted huge signs in whitewash: "Onward Slaves of Moscow", "Onward you Jitterbugging Bastards", "You Want Berlin, Moscow Gets It". Some enterprising GIs had painted the Third Army's ubiquitous reply: "Kilroy Was Here". Speaking of ubiquity, at Yalta, Stalin returned from a head-call and told an aide: "Find out who Kilroy is". In World War II, wherever the U.S.Military went, and that was everywhere, if nature called, somewhere on the shithouse wall, you would find Kilroy's laconic missive.

Like the Alpenstrasse, the Mosel is lined with storybook towns and castles. The Mosel snakes it way through a valley of deeply slopped vineyards. Like the Alpenstrasse, the towns along its banks are filled with fabulous hotels, inns, restaurants, weinstubes (wine bars) and boutiques. Many of the towns have ancient castles towering over them. Some, like Cochem's Reichburg, rival Neuschwanstein in baroque ostentation. Other nearby castles are: Marienburg in Alf, Metternich in Beilstein, and Burg Eltz in Moselkern.

The Mosel flows into the Rhein at Koblenz. This is called 'Deutches Eck" (Germany's Corner). Technically, the "Rhineland" is the 50-mile section of the river between Koblenz and Mainz. The swift-flowing Rhine Gorge is the 20-kilometer section between Boppard and Oberwesel. This is where the Third Army assaulted the river in March 1945. Patton selected the Rhine Gorge because: "the impossible place is usually the least well defended". The high vineyard walls lining both banks are the source of it's wealth and beauty. Above the town of St. Goar stand the ruins of Berg Rheinfels, the largest and most famous castle on the Rhein. Across the river lies the sister town of St Goarhausen, with its own castles, Katz and Maus.

The famous Lorelei rocks are just up stream on the St Goarhausen side, between St. Goar and Oberwesel. Burg Rheinfels has been partially restored and converted into a posh hotel. There is a panoramic dining room and balcony that looks down on the towns and the Lorelei. From Bernkastel-Kues to St. Goar is about a 60-kilometer drive, mainly on Route 327.

Tweet

Tweet came into our lives on a spring day, around noon at Dupont Circle. Traffic was bumper to bumper. I spotted a baby bird hunkered-down in the middle of the street with a life expectancy of millisecond. I stopped the car in front of her, blocking the traffic. I put her on a towel in the front seat beside me and headed home. She sat quietly watching me the whole trip home. She was imprinting me. At home, I put her down on the carpet in the living room and went to the kitchen to get her some water. A sixth sense told me to look down. She had followed me into the kitchen and was standing by my foot. From that point she followed me everywhere. Tweet was a baby female robin. At first her feathers were short, but as they grew she began to do short take offs and landings, gradually increasing flight times. She got in the habit of orbiting me and landing on top of my head. She would come when you called her. We would whistle, she would whistle back, and come flying in. She ate live meal worms like popcorn; also earthworms and small bugs.

At night, she would sit on the arm of your chair watching TV or listening to music. She often bobbed up and down to the rhythmn . Whatever we were drinking, she had to "wet her beak" ; ice tea, beer or bubbly. After imbibing, she would fly up to a valance to sleep it off. When Vicki and I went upstairs to bed we would whistle, she would answer, and come flying upstairs to her pillow in the bookcase behind the bed. She was a self-taught social butterfly; always completely at ease with our guests. When I worked at my desk, she would sit and watch me or take a nap. Female Robins can open their breast feathers like a bomb-bay door to keep eggs warm. We sometimes put Tweet in a large cage that sat in front of the rear window looking out over the woods. The land behind our house is State Park. In the summer, a large male Robin took up sentry duty in the large Dogwood limb just outside the window. We called him Hood. Hood an Tweet held loquacious conferences. Tweet had grown into a beautiful young thing and Hood was a handsome rascal. We reluctantly decided to set her free.

We took the cage to the upstairs deck and opened the door. Hood was waiting on a nearby Hickory limb. She flew up to Hood, then flew back down and orbited us. Tweet and Hood flew away. A lot of Robins hang around our Alpine House, we wonder if some of them are Tweets kids. Maybe we're just well know among Robins as "Special Friends of Robins".

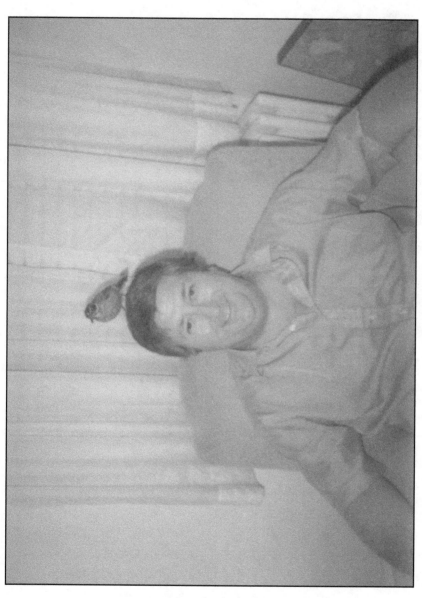

Tweet–Tweet

Heidi

Flying Squirrels are the cutest animals on the planet. They are really tiny; about half the size of a Chipmunk. In Colonial times people carried them around in their pockets, like a baby Roo. Heidi got into my house through a tiny hole in my porch roof. Heidi was highly skilled infiltrator; small quick dashes from cover to cover. While reading or watching TV, I caught glimpses of something very tiny and fast working its way closer as in "The Little Prince". When she stopped in the open, I realized she was a Flying-Squirrel from my scouting days. She graduated from eating nuts in front of the chair to eating them out of my hand. For those who may wonder, it is very easy to distinguish male and female squirrels. She was the most beautiful creature I've ever seen. Snow-white belly, with reddish-brown trim line, topped by a gray back, tiny paws. Realizing she needed a warm, secure home for the Winter, I cut a small hole in the end of a shoe box and filled it with socks. Her favorite food were slices of apple and pecans. I placed Heidi's Alpine hut atop the kitchen cabinets. She slept days, but made social forays in the evening. She departed in the Spring.

Heidi

Shelter

I always hoped God had a job for me. When I was a teenager, I wanted to be Billy Sunday-type evangelist. Alas, I never came upon a burning bush. However, I've always been obsessed with the plight of the homeless. Nobody on the planet should have to sleep outdoors in the winter. In late 1982, I became interested in Mitch Snyder, who headed a group called Community for Creative Non Violence (CCNV). They had taken over an abandoned federal building at 425 2nd Street, NW (now Mitch Snyder Place) and turned it into a homeless shelter. I decided to write a musical about a homeless shelter. I began to visit CCNV and other shelters in the area to gather material. When I met Mitch his first question to me was: "How many pairs of shoes do you own?" It's an interesting question. How much of the stuff that you own do you really need? The next day I gave my L.L. Bean hunting boots to the shelter. Through relentless fasting and crusading, Mitch was able to convert the facility into the largest shelter (1400-beds) in Washington, DC.

I decided to name my musical *Shelter*. Ernie Joselovitz, President for life of the Playwrights Forum arranged for a staged reading by equity actors at a theater in Old Town Alexandria. I made a CD of the music. Art Lisi, who did the music for the Cosby Show, arranged the music. Students from the Levine School of Music did the vocals. Occasionally, I dig it out to revise it or to try to get someone interested in staging it.

SHELTER

BOOK, WORDS & MUSIC
by
JIM EDWARDS

SHELTER

Book, Words and Music
by
Jim Edwards

James B. Edwards
2923 North 24th Street
Arlington, VA 22207
703-527-4775

Copyright 2011

SHELTER

SYNOPSIS

On any cold winter night, with rain or snow falling relentlessly upon them, the armies of the
homeless, bent and broken, march aimlessly to nowhere - their only destination - the night's end.
This is a musical about a battle for shelter. Hutch Hutcheson has converted an abandoned
building into a shelter. He wants to create a model facility for the homeless; Ann Harding helps.
Mike Murphy is a mysterious stranger who shows up to help run the shelter. Joe Williams and
Willie Hackett are veterans living at the shelter; out of work and down on their luck. Irving
Winston VII is a tragicomic schizophrenic, who strides around the shelter, ranting about
ridiculous conspiracies.

Conway Construction has bought and bulldozed the area around the shelter; they plan to build a
shopping mall. The shelter is the only building still standing on their tract. City Hall has
condemned the property and is trying to shut it down. Hutch is trying to move to a vacant hotel -
the Excelcior. He wants to convert it to a model shelter, named for the cheapest property on the
Monopoly board - the Mediterranean. The climax is a midnight showdown with the police in a
snowstorm.

CAST COSTUMES STAGING

Hutch Hutcheson is the crusader type; the shelter is his crusade.
Ann Harding is educated and pretty; with a touch of Tomboy.
Mike Murphy is a mysterious stranger; educated, articulate, widely traveled; he may be an angel
or an extraterrestrial.
Joe Williams is a veteran; cynical and intelligent.
Willie Hackett is a veteran; good natured, tough, and streetwise.
Irving Winston VII is a large, imposing man. He wears a purple overcoat and a derby covered
with gold stars. He is a schizophrenic with outrageous delusions of grandeur.
Dan Wilson is a reporter for the Washington Times; doing a story on the shelter.

Except for Wilson and Winston, the cast wear war surplus uniforms.
Except for the scene in Ann's apartment, all scenes take place in one lobby and office set.

MUSIC

OVERTURE
LONESOME
GOD NEEDS SOME HELP ALONG THE WAY
CASTLES IN THE AIR
WHY AIN'T THERE NOTHIN FOR ME
SUMP'UMS GAININ ON YOU
DOESN'T ANYONE CARE
JUST SOME HELP FROM YOU

OVERTURE

ACT 1 - SCENE 1

Curtain closed; stage dark. Front center stage, Willie and Joe are huddled over the fire in an oil drum. Rubbing their hands; passing a bottle; they sing: LONESOME.

WILLIE: It's too damn cold - gotta get another bottle.
JOE: How much do we need?
WILLIE: A buck would do it.
JOE: I think I see it coming.

A figure approaches, wearing a hooded duffle coat; carrying a rucksack.

STRANGER: Hey guys - name's Mike - lookin for a shelter near here - know where it is?
WILLIE: D street - coupla blocks from here.
JOE: Don't happen to have a spare buck?
WILLIE: That's all we need for another jug.
MIKE: Gonna get really cold tonight - why don't you guys show me the way to that shelter?
WILLIE: We heard about it.
MIKE: What'd you hear?
JOE: Heard it's a zoo.
MIKE: Why don't we go there and improve the clientele?
JOE: We don't go for the Mission scene, Mister.
MIKE: Might not be like that - just three hots and a cot. Goin down to 20 degrees!
JOE: 20 degrees!
MIKE: What they say - maybe we can make chowtime.
JOE: What the hell - whatta you think Willie?
WILLIE: Right - let's get these troops in outta the hot sun!

Light goes out in oil drum; players exit; drum and tree removed. Curtain opens on shelter lobby.

Shelter lobby. Hutch is sitting at a desk, registering guests. It is snowing heavily outside the double-door entrance at rear center stage. There are large signs painted on the walls at left and right rear stage.

CLUB MED
BREAKFAST: 7 - 9
LUNCH: 12 - 2
DINNER: 6 -8

NO WEAPONS
NO FIGHTING

Mike, Willie and Joe enter; brushing off snow.

HUTCH: The Three Musketeers - welcome aboard - name's Hutch - I try to run this circus!
JOE: Hi Hutch - I'm Joe - this is my buddy Willie.
HUTCH: Joe - Willie - welcome aboard - I'll put you guys in 110 (writes in ledger). Pick up your blankets at supply down the hall. You can still make chow in the basement. We're noted for our stew!
MIKE: Hi Hutch - name's Mike Murphy. An old friend of yours said to look you up.
HUTCH: Who?
MIKE: Tom Murray at the Baltic in San Diego.
HUTCH: You know Tom?
MIKE: Helped him out at the Baltic.
HUTCH: Fantastic - welcome aboard - take 112 Mike - it's a single. After you chow down come by for coffee - want to hear all about Tom and the Baltic.

Irving Winston VII enters wearing a purple coat and derby with gold stars all over it. He stops in front of one of the men leaning against the wall, takes a crumpled note from his pocket and hands it to the man. Man unfolds the note, reads it with a perplexed look on his face.

MAN: What the shit is this?
IRVING: WHAT THE SHIT IS THIS - YOUR GRACE!

Irving wheels away and strolls majestically past the desk.

HUTCH: How goes it this evening, your Grace?
IRVING: THINGS ARE OUT OF CONTROL!
HUTCH: You can say that again (Irving stops and glares) YOUR GRACE!

Irving walks over to a man dozing against the wall.

IRVING: (His loud voice causes the man to jump off the floor) RUSSIAN SPETZNAZ CONTROL INDIAN FAMILIES! CHINESE INTERFACE WITH FOREIGN GOVERNMENTS!
MAN: You crazy son-of-a-bitch - what the hell you supposed to be?
IRVING: IRVING WINSTON THE SEVENTH, PRESIDENT, KING, PROTECTOR OF MEXICO! IF YOU ARE ADDRESSING ME - USE MY TITLE - YOUR GRACE!
MAN: Crazy asshole!
IRVING: CRAZY ASSHOLE - YOUR GRACE!

SCENE 2

Hutch and Mike are drinking coffee in the office.

HUTCH: Well, Mike, looks like you've been everywhere – seen everything – like you're on some kind of quest.
MIKE: Man's ancient quest for knowledge and wisdom, Hutch. Sometimes, I seem to be making progress. Other times, I just seem to be collecting a lotta data. Stuff like – did you know that if you hold a penny at arms length, you block out three galaxies from your view! And those galaxies are 350 million light-years away!
HUTCH: Fantastic! I read an article that said that the common housefly contains one million atoms for every second of time since the age of the dinosaurs!
MIKE: Looks like the work of an incredibly intelligent designer, doesn't it!
HUTCH: A fantastic engineer! Coming back down to earth, bring me up to date on the Baltic.
MIKE: Well, as you know, every room is like a small hotel room – bed, shower, toilet, washbasin, chair and lamp. They have an outpatient clinic with volunteer doctors. Like most shelters, they get their food gratis from grocery stores, wholesalers, restaurants. Baltic tries to help every resident get some kind of job. They have training classes in everything from how to dress and act for a job interview to introduction to computers. They arrange trial jobs – dishwashers, laborers, clerks, sometimes executives – some of these people have fallen from high places. Everybody pays Baltic a flat 10% of their wages – some months Baltic even makes a profit! But tell me, Hutch, how can I help you out here?
HUTCH: We've got two problems, Mike. The first is Conway Construction. They're going to build a mall here. They bought and bulldozed the surrounding area. They bought City Hall. City Hall harasses us about code violations – closing the kitchen – turning off the heat – they want us outta here. We keep begging for time to find a new place. We want to get the old Excelsior and convert it into a Baltic. Which brings us to Silas Flynt.
MIKE: Who's Silas Flynt?
HUTCH: He owns the Excelsior.
MIKE: Tell me about Silas Flynt.
HUTCH: I haven't been able to see him. Everybody says he's like Henry F. Potter in It's a Wonderful Life. But like Dr. Chumley in Harvey – Silas Flynt sees no one!
MIKE: Maybe Silas is the key. In my long sojourn, I've found folks are usually a lot better than other folks say they are. Let me try to see Silas Flynt.
HUTCH: Fantastic Mike – maybe you're our key!

Hutch and Mike sing: GOD NEEDS SOME HELP ALONG THE WAY.

Mike puts on his coat – exits with a wave and a smile.

MIKE: Guess I'll go check the grates!

SCENE 3

The office. Hutch is on one phone; Ann on another.

HUTCH: Some say there are 500 homeless in the city - others say 10,000 (pause) what do the experts say? Those are the experts!
ANN: People are pouring in - we need more cots and blankets.
HUTCH: It costs us about $10 per person per day (pause). Expensive! It costs the jail $50 per!
ANN: Could you let us have 100 more cots and blankets?
HUTCH: Half of them are mental patients - thrown in the street when all the asylums were shut down.
ANN: Ann Harding, Mr. Simons. This awful weather - people are pouring in. We need meat and veggies for the stew.
HUTCH: The shelters need outpatient clinics to treat the schizos and manics.
ANN: Chicken works - thank you, Mr. Simons.
HUTCH: Thousands are freezing and starving - murdered by indifference.

They finish talking at the same time.

ANN: How's the bill doing?
HUTCH: Still in committee. How'd you do?
ANN: Mr. Hulbert can let us have the cots and blankets. Mr. Simons is low on beef, so he's sending chicken.
HUTCH: We'll make do. The Brazilians say: "If you don't have a dog - hunt with your cat."
MIKE: (entering) Can I bum a cuppa - far from the madding crowd?
ANN: Help yourself.

Irving Winston VII comes to the door.

IRVING: MOVING SOON TO PALACE MANSION! INHERITED RULED MONIES!
WORLDWIDE CONFLICT AGAINST POLITICAL STRUCTURES! (Irving strides away)

MIKE: Think I'll talk to Irving - maybe I can help him.
ANN: That would be a miracle.
MIKE: Remember Flower Drum Song: "a hundred million miracles are happening every day."
ANN: Mike, how long since you had a home-cooked meal?
MIKE: Ages!
ANN: Grab your coat - we'll go to my place for Scallopini.
MIKE: As Hutch says: Fantastic!

SCENE 4

Ann's apartment. As curtain opens, Ann is playing a small piano; she and Mike are singing Avalon.

MIKE: Did you know Avalon is the Celtic word for Atlantis - the land of make-believe.

ANN: We could both use some beach-time there. What do you think this circus is all about Mike?

MIKE: Maybe our computers - our brains - are too primitive to comprehend the really big stuff. Maybe we're like a pack of wild dogs running loose in the Library of Congress. The knowledge of the world is all around them - but not one of the pack has the computer power to pull down a book and read. Maybe our limits are programmed in. Maybe that's why we've never been able to get anything right - primative computers. But then - this is just a tiny planet in a tiny galaxy. Did you know that if there were only three bees in the entire United States - the air would be more crowded with bees than space is with galaxies?

ANN: That's incredible! So - what is Mike Murphy looking for in this vast universe?

MIKE: I'd settle for a better world right here. Maybe we should start building castles again like King Ludwig of Bavaria.

ANN: He was crazy, wasn't he?

MIKE: Maybe he was sane and the world was nuts! With the same amount of effort, we could have made life on this planet a Romberg operetta - instead of what we have made it - a Kafka nightmare!

ANN: So we should build castles like Ludwig?

MIKE: Be better than what we've done so far.

ANN: Be a little expensive, wouldn't it?

MIKE: Expensive! With the oceans of money governments have squandered down through the ages on the madness of wars - slaughtering people by the hundreds of millions - all the world could be living in castles!

ANN: And wear costumes!

MIKE: And sing beautiful songs at each other!

ANN: Have to have background music!

MIKE: Life should always have background music!

Ann and Mike sing: CASTLES IN THE AIR.

Evolves into Astaire/Rogers dance number as scene ends.

Curtain. End of Act I.

SCENE 5

Lobby. Joe and Willie are leaning against a wall talking.

JOE: That Murphy's a strange bird isn't he?
WILLIE: Seems like he's been everywhere.
JOE: Seems like he's from another planet.
WILLIE: Reminds me of an old priest I met once.
JOE: Irving seems to be getting better since Mike started talking to him.
WILLIE: Yeah, some of the stuff he shouts is starting to make sense.
JOE: Hey buddy, we gotta find some work.
WILLIE: Heard about a corner near here where you can get day work - you know about it?
JOE: You wouldn't like. *it*
WILLIE: How come?
JOE: It's mean work. You work for the eviction man. Ride around in a truck, puttin peoples stuff in the street - they're hollering and crying. It's mean work!
WILLIE: Any other work we can get?
JOE: Builders always need laborers.
WILLIE: Trouble with day labor, you gotta work at it regular or it'll kill you.
JOE: And if you work regular you gotta join the union.
WILLIE: What's that cost?
JOE: About 300 bucks - last I heard.
WILLIE: 300 bucks - so much for that.
JOE: What we need is a job where you're your own boss - like owning a cab.
WILLIE: Now you're talking!
JOE: We could look for a "mechanics special" to fix up - take turns running it.
WILLIE: Hey, I like that!
JOE: Get us back on our feet.

Joe and Willie sing: WHY AIN'T THERE NOTHIN FOR ME?

As the scene ends, Mike and Irving pass in the background, quietly talking.

SCENE 6

Lobby and office. Ann is at the front desk. Hutch and Mike are waiting in the office. Man enters goes to front desk.

MAN: I'm Dan Wilson - Washington Times - I have an appointment with Hutcheson and Murphy.
ANN: I'm Ann Harding. They're waiting for you there in the office.
WILSON: Thank you Ann. (walks over to office) Dan Wilson - Washington Times.
HUTCH: I'm Hutch Hutcheson, this is Mike Murphy.
WILSON: I've heard most of the people here prefer the street or a shelter to working. They know how to flim-flam the welfare system and spend all their panhandling money on booze and drugs.
HUTCH: Homelessness has a hundred causes - mental illness, drugs, alcohol, busted marriages, illiteracy, bad luck, hard times. If you want to know what caused homelessness, start with three ten dollar words - deinstitutionalism, deindustrialization, and urban-renewal. All over America mental institutions were shut down and the patients were thrown in the street - 85% of the homeless are schizos, bi-polars, alkis, or addicts. Deindustrialization costs America millions of good paying jobs. There used to be plenty of work in factories, shipyards, railroads, mines. Every big city had slum-housing and flea-bag hotels where you could get a room for a dollar a night. Government social-engineers tore down over a million of these facilities all across America. It was called "urban-renewal." To top it all off, the government perpetuated poverty by subsidizing it!
MIKE: The government caused this whole damn mess. Congress should be required to wear clown costumes and play circus music when they're in session! Government has no right to send one nickel to a foreign country as long as one American is hungry or homeless! Not one American should sleep without a roof over his head! Every town and city has empty factories, warehouses, storefronts. America's ports have thousands of mothballed ships that could house the poor and homeless.
WILSON: Hey, I like the idea of Congress in clown suits! Think I'll do a column on it! How the hell did you guys get in the shelter game?
HUTCH: OK- without a lotta personal stuff - I got down and out and couldn't make the rent. That's when I spent my first night in a shelter. You had to line up in the snow to wait for it to open. The shelter had a guy we called "Gorgeous George" - looked like a shaved ape! George used a nightstick to keep the guests in line. They had rules about everything. George and his "stern but kindly" helpers made sure you obeyed them. One night George threw an old guy outta line for coughing too much. I went to the old guys defense and George did some on-the-spot dental work on me with his stick. The next day the old guy was found frozen to death. So I joined some guys on a heat grate. We used to sit looking at all the empty buildings - wishing we could go sit in the basements - anywhere out of that cold. Then one night it came to me - we'd take over an empty building and set up a shelter. That's what we did! This is the place!
WILSON: Thanks guys - think I'll go write that clown column! RIGHT THIS WAY - LADEEEZ AND GENTLEMEEEN!!

Wilson exits to circus music.

SCENE 7

Joe and Willie are huddled in the lobby, wrapped in blankets. Irving Winston VII walks up, takes
a stack of notes from his pocket, hands one to Willie, and begins shouting.

IRVING: CALL FBI AND CIA STAFF! SUSPECT ARRESTED ON FEDERAL VIOLATION
WARRANT! TIC-TAC DEVICES ACTIVATE ALL TELEPHONES! VOICES ARE HEARD
BY ALL WHO ENTER!

Irving wheels and strides away. Willie studies the note; hands it to Joe.

WILLIE: Hey partner – can you read this – makes no sense to me.
JOE: (studying note) I can read it – makes no sense to me either.
WILLIE: This place is crammed with crazies.
JOE: Another case of the road to hell and good intentions.
WILLIE: How's that?
JOE: Years ago the ACLU decided the crazies rights were being trampled on in the looney bins.
So the ACLU got Congress to pass laws shutting down all the asylums and throwing all the
patients in the street. So all over America the crazies ended up on the heat grates!
WILLIE: Man – that is world class cruelty!
JOE: Speaking of cruelty, I heard Murphy talking about one of Stalin's prisons. Place called
Sukhanovka. At Sukhanovka, they never stopped beating the prisoners – 24/7/365 – the
screaming never stopped! Murphy said anybody sent to Sukhanovka was killed or driven mad!
Nobody came out alive or sane! He said it was the worst example of cruelty in the history of the
world! He's trying to get somebody to do a movie about it. Did you ever notice there is no
commandment about cruelty?
WILLIE: Yeah – that's right. Lotta stuff about coveting neighbors wives.
JOE: Lotta stuff about graven images – nothing about cruelty! The Romans spent 500 years
killing people for entertainment – mass murder for laughs!
WILLIE: Nothin in there about hate either.
JOE: Could have come up with a better set of rules on the back of an envelope!
WILLIE: Hey Joe – let's talk about something else – like the cab business.
JOE: Murphy knows about vet's benefits – maybe he could help us get a loan.
WILLIE: Think he could?
JOE: Cost nothing to ask. Been thinking about a name. How does WILJO CAB grab you?
WILLIE: WILJO CAB! Right on!
JOE: Let's go talk to Murphy.
WILLIE: I'm right behind you Joe!

Joe and Willie sing: SUMPIN'S GAININ ON YOU.

SCENE 8

Hutch and Mike wait in the office. Reporter Wilson enters.

WILSON: Hi guys - sorry I'm late - it's raining cats and dogs out there!
HUTCH: Yeah - a real Army day!
WILSON: I need to get more historical background on the homeless.
HUTCH: OK - I'll start - chime in anytime Mike. In Gay 90s London, the Salvation Army offered a menu of shelters. For a penny, you could get a "penny sit-up", where you were allowed to sit, but not sleep, on a wooden bench. For two pennies, there was the "two penny hangover." It had a rope strung in front of a wooden bench that you could hang over. The rope was cut at sunrise to encourage the guests to wake up and hit the street. For four pennies, you could bask in a spa called a "coffin house." There you could sleep in a coffin shaped box, warm and cozy under a canvas tarp. Tell him about Gay 90s America, Mike.
MIKE: In Gay 90s America, for a nickel a night, you could get a cot in a "flophouse" - a big room with heat - if you were lucky. For a dime, you could move upscale to a dorm. Here you got bedding, a locker, and a washbasin to take a "whore's bath". These "fleabags" were private businesses. The manager could throw out troublemakers - which is more than you can do today in public shelters or public schools! A major problem today is the disappearance of the old shape-up gangs at the docks, railroads, factories. Anybody could get a days work just by showing up. There was no commitment - a big problem for alkis and druggies. During America's great railroad and industrial expansion, every city had a large number of "flophouses" and "fleabags" - really cheap shelter! And they made money - no subsidies - no tax breaks!
HUTCH: The point is - the homeless in the Gay 90s and the Great Depression were better off than they are today! The cheapest "fleabag" beats the hell out of a cardboard box! Some of today's mayors are straight out of Dickens! One Ft. Lauderdale mayor had the city's trash cans sprayed with insecticide. His honor said: "The best way to get rid of vermin is to cut off their food supply." New York city's billionaire mayor charges homeless people half their earnings to stay in a city shelter - pay up or "hit the sidewalk."
MIKE: We need to bring back "fleabag" hotels. San Diego's Baltic could be a model for the future. It's named for the cheapest property on the Monopoly board. The rooms have a bed, sink, toilet, and there's shower room on each floor. The rent is cheap - but they make money. We're trying to get hold of the old Excelsior on 14th street; it's vacant and boarded up. We want to make it like the Baltic and name it after the other cheap property on the Monopoly board - the Mediterranean.
WILSON: Do you think most of these people can take care of a place like that?
HUTCH: They do at the Baltic. Let's give them a chance. Some of these people come out of environments you can't imagine. They were not raised in a house or apartment - they grew up in a room. The bathroom and kitchen were down the hall - shared with the other roomers. They lived with their mother and four or five half brothers and sisters. Their mother was a third generation welfare illiterate who never worked a day in her life. Because of the welfare system's "man in the house rule" their father could not live with their mother. Usually, the only man they saw was a "Welfare Pimp" - guys who have a string of welfare mothers they extort money from every month. I'll finish by saying that if the government had hired the Ku Klux Klan to design the welfare system, they could not have come up with a better plan to destroy Black society!

SCENE 9

Hutch and Ann are in the office, drinking coffee; Mike enters.

HUTCH: Well Mike - tell us about the meeting with the elusive Silas Flynt.
ANN: What's he really like? What does he look like?
MIKE: Silas Flynt is no Henry Potter. He's highly educated, widely traveled, extremely interesting. He's 88, but looks 60.
ANN: What did you talk about?
MIKE: Everything - ships and shoes and sealing wax, cabbages and kings. We talked about how One Day on the Heat Grates is like Solzhenitsyn's One Day in the Life of Ivan Denisovich. A fight to survive another day. We talked about how each of us changes the world - the "Butterfly Effect"!
HUTCH: Or the George Bailey effect from It's a Wonderful Life!
MIKE: Right.
HUTCH: What about the Excelsior?
MIKE: It's complicated. How will the shelter impact the area. How may he may be able to help.
ANN: Do you think he'll do it?
MIKE: I'm optimistic. Meanwhile, let's try to find the key to Conway Construction.
HUTCH: Yeah - they're our biggest problem.
MIKE: Ever stop to think how big a problem we are for them?
ANN: That's true!
MIKE: Maybe our approach should be - how can we help each other.
HUTCH: Right - that's supposed to be our stock in trade!
MIKE: Maybe my work here is almost finished.
ANN:(looking alarmed) We need you here Mike!
MIKE: There are still a lot of heat grates out there.

SCENE 10

Lobby. People are carrying boxes around; some are going out the door with their belongings in shopping bags. Joe and Willie are sitting on their duffel bags, watching.

WILLIE: Man, I'm about to freeze!
JOE: Beats the grates!
WILLIE: Sure - also beats a foxhole!
JOE: Or a minefield - see things could be worse.
WILLIE: Still - somebody ought to shoot that damn Mayor!
JOE: First the kitchen, now the heat.
WILLIE: Looks like they're really gonna shut us down this time.
JOE: Nobody gives a damn!
WILLIE: Thought we were going to the Excelsior.
JOE: Mike was working on it.
WILLIE: Looks like the deal fell through.
 JOE: Everybody smells blood - they're trying to finish us off.
WILLIE: They're gonna force us in that city shelter.
JOE: His honor spent a lotta money on it - can't let it set vacant.
WILLIE: It's a prison - nobody will go - we'll be back on the grates.
JOE: Nobody cares!

Joe and Willie sing: DOESN'T ANYONE CARE?

Curtain. End of Act II.

ACT III - SCENE 11

Shelter lobby. Nightime. Snow is blowing in through open lobby doors. Hutch, Ann and Mike, Joe and Willie are in the doorway facing outside. Hutch and Mike have bullhorns. Irving paces back and forth; now and then going to the door to shout something. Rest of cast scattered around the lobby.

POLICE CAPTAIN (voice outside with bullhorn): This is the police captain, I have orders to take possession of this property at midnight. All of you people must come out of the building.
HUTCH (with bullhorn): My God, man - it's 20 degrees and snowing!
CAPTAIN: We have buses to take you to the City's shelter.
HUTCH: Police buses!
MIKE: People of America - don't let this happen! They are going to tear down the only home these people have!
ANN: They will be back on the heat grates!
IRVING: GOD WILL AVENGE!
CAPTAIN: They are being moved to the City's shelter.
JOE: The City's Gulag!
WILLIE: Tell 'em Joe!
HUTCH: In God's name don't do this. This is the only home they have!
MIKE: Most of these men are veterans. They fought to save all of you from death camps and the Gulag!
ANN: They deserve better than this!
IRVING: VENGENCE IS MINE SAYETH THE LORD!
CAPTAIN: It is now midnight! I have a court order to take possession of this facility. Please come out of the building.
MIKE: "Inasmuch as ye have done it unto the least of these, ye have done it unto me"!
ANN: "You are your brother's keeper"!
IRVING: GOD WILL RAIN DOWN FIRE AND BRIMSTONE UPON YOU!

At this moment, sirens scream and police lights flash.

POLICE CHIEF (with bullhorn): This is the chief of the District Police Department! All law enforcement personnel stand down immediately! I have a court order to stop these proceedings!

Roar goes up from the shelter people. Mike and Hutch, then all around them, fall to their knees.

Cast sings: JUST SOME HELP FROM YOU.

SCENE 12 FINALE

The shelter is having a big party celebrating the move to the Excelsior/Mediterranean. Media people are videotaping the event. Irving Winston VII moves among the crowd shaking hands and smiling. Joe and Willie are wearing chauffer caps with a badge saying: WILJO CAB. Hutch is finishing a speech.

HUTCH: Let me finish by saying the Med is going to be a model for cities all across America. It's a giant step in providing affordable housing for the homeless. Let's join the party!

HUTCH: Wiljo Cab - how goes the cab business?
JOE: We're working on another "mechanics special."
WILLIE: It's almost ready.
HUTCH: Fantastic!
MIKE: Watch out Yellow Cab!
HUTCH: Hey everybody - here's to Wiljo Cab! To all the losers of the world - today they won one!
MIKE: The Bible says they will win them all in the end - "the last shall be first."
HUTCH: Let's all drink to that. (cast toasts)
ANN: Let's all drink to Mike and Hutch - they're the ones who did it!
MIKE: Don't forget Silas Flynt and the Conrad people.
(cast toasts Mike and Hutch)
ANN: Now that you saved us - are you going to stick around awhile?
MIKE: Shall we dance?

Ann and Mike begin dancing to: CASTLES IN THE AIR.

Show ends with cast singing: SUMPIN'S GAINING ON YOU.

LONESOME

Wor ds and Music by
JIM EDWARDS

March ing all through the night____ go - ing no - wheres, All a -
wan - der - ing aim - less____ and worn down, Roam ing

lone in a world____ where____ no one cares. Some are bent un - der des - pair____ and
blea - ry - eyed all____ o - ver down town. All day look-ing in fac - es____ that

sad - ness, oth - ers driv - en by dead____ dreams____ to mad - ness
speak hate, All night try - ing to sleep____ on____ a heat grate.

CHORUS

Lone - some hun - gry and bent with des - pair,

All hope is long since past. Pray - ing to - nights the

last.____ 2.Out there last.

GOD NEEDS SOME HELP ALONG THE WAY

Words by:JIM EDWARDS
Music by : ARTHUR SULLIV

1.Life is a jour - ney long___ and far
2.Life is a strug - gle all of the way
3.Some - times the path is rock - y and steep.

Hard as a pil - gri - mage to a star
some of us fall and wan - der a stray
Some - times the wat - ers tur - bid and deep.

Act as a guide a - cross the bar
God needs some help a - long the way
Reach out and save some soul to - day.

light up the cor - ner where you are
show He can count on you to day.
God needs some help a - long the way.

CASTLES IN THE AIR

Words and Music by
JIM EDWARDS

1.Come live with me in dream - land where life's an op - er -
2.This life could be a toy - land where ev - 'ry dream comes
3.We're a perf - ect coup - le All the world can

et - ta.   Where   mu - sic in the back - ground
true,____   If   on - ly you would let me
see,____   hap - py as a porpoise pair

col - - - ors, the li - bret - - - ta.
spend____ all of it with you.
play - in' in the sea.____

REFRAIN
Mock - ing birds are sing - ing,   love is ev' - ry - where,

but - ter cups and dais - ies,   Cas - tles in the air. *(Last Time Fine)*

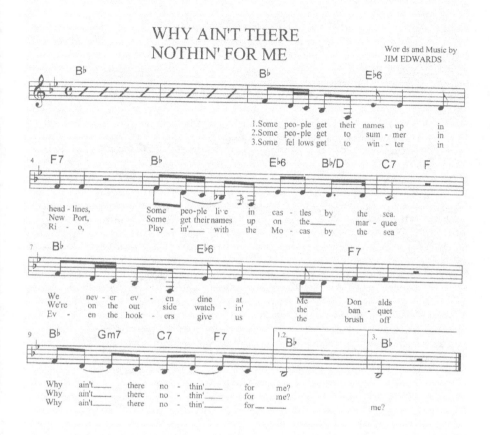

WHY AIN'T THERE
NOTHIN' FOR ME

Words and Music by
JIM EDWARDS

Sump'ums Gainin on you
(you can't take it with you)

Words and Music by
JIM EDWARDS

1.If you find each day is more like Kaf - ka and ain;t no fun at all,___ and you're miss - in' all the joy and laugh - ta and life just ain't a ball.___ Don't col - lect no junk an' pack your pock - ets, you can:t take it with you,___ don't look back, there;s sump - um gain - in' on you. 2.Make your

2.Make your mind up that you've fin - 'ly had___ it and then just walk a - way,___ Get a - way from all the phon - ey climb - ers and come on out and play,___ Leave the rat race to the bot - tom li - ners and don't look back of you.___ And cause you're you're sure to find that sump - ums___ gain - in'.___ on

DOESN'T ANYONE CARE

Words and Music by
JIM EDWARDS

On a cold win - ter ev - ening,
Bro - ken heart - ed and hun - gry,
In a world filled with sad - ness,
Does - n't an - y - one care?

When you're warm in your bed,
He keeps march - ing no - where,
Doub - le - deal - ing and hate,
Does - n't an - y - one care?

Stop and think of your
Cry - ing soft - ly to
show you care for some -
Peo - ple sleep - ing on

broth - er,
Heav - en
bo - dy,
heat grates,

with no place for his head.
Does - n't an - y - one care?
be - fore it is too late.
Does - n't an - y - one

care?

JUST SOME HELP FROM YOU

Words: JIM EDWARDS
Music: Traditional

©1984Jim Edwards

Good News Television, Inc.

In 2004, I formed a corporation to try to get a new type of television programming off the ground. I contacted and mailed letters to a broad spectrum of people like : Phillip Anschutz, Brian Lamb, George Lucas, Laura Bush, Colin Powell. If implemented, it would have revolutionized the industry. I was willing to keep plugging away at the cultural crusade for years. Unfortunately, the bureaucracy of the State Corporation Commission finally did me in with incessant requirements of minutia, deadlines, etc. The problem has metastasized. Today, suffocation by malignant pandemic government bureaucracy is the greatest threat to our Republic.

STATE CORPORATION COMMISSION

Richmond, September 15, 2004

This is to certify that the certificate of incorporation of

Good News Television, Inc.

was this day issued and admitted to record in this office and that the said corporation is authorized to transact its business subject to all Virginia laws applicable to the corporation and its business. Effective date: September 15, 2004

State Corporation Commission
Attest:

_____
Clerk of the Commission

Every night American television audiences are drowned in an ocean of obscenity, violence, murders, wars, famines, plagues, tornadoes, droughts; and unrelenting deluge of calamity and despair. The wonder is that the entire country has not been driven into hopeless depression or madness. A growing number of viewers are "turned off" by this metastasizing electronic nightmare. Watching television one would think that nothing constructive, beautiful, fascinating, and wonderful is going on anywhere in the world. When, in fact, the opposite is true; we live in a world where " a hundred million miracles are happening every day."

America and the world need a "Good News Network"(GNN) featuring only constructive and happy events and developments. The programming possibilities are literally unlimited. GNN will revolutionize education and entertainment. GNN will trigger a worldwide renaissance in learning and morality. Some random programming possibilities:

- Attending lectures by the top university professors in the world in all academic disciplines: science, history, philosophy, art, literature, music, etc.
- Dropping in on "The Season" in Palm Beach; "Carnaval" in Rio; "Oktoberfest" in Munich.
- Visiting famous plays and musicals.
- Visiting great museums and galleries.
- Visiting famous restaurants of the world.
- Visiting the homes of the rich and famous .
- Visiting the annual top fashion shows.
- Watching the world's top decorators at work.

- Examining the Atomic Aircraft: Powered by a hafnium-fueled reactor, unmanned, it would be able to stay aloft indefinitely.
- Taking a look at Zero Point Energy (ZPE): Hypersonic megaliners – 1200 passengers, 12,000 miles in 70 minutes.
- Visiting Burt Rutan's low cost orbital vehicle – Space Ship One or his Globalflyer – one man, one engine, around the world nonstop in 80 hours.
- Looking at General Motors revolutionary"Autonomy", a modular fuel cell

th interchangeable bodies to suit your mood or needs.
- Taking another look at GM's 1991 "Ultralite" that weighed 1400 pounds, could carry four passengers at 135 mph, and average 100mpg – 200 mpg as a hybrid.
- Looking at the future of robotics, like powered exoskeletons for the handicapped.
- Classic Cars Review: In depth history and analysis of famous cars, such as the 1938 D8 120 "Delahaye" Delage with coachwork by Letourneur et Marchand.

There are others striving for a renaissance in the television industry. A group of leading scientists is launching Cable Science Network (CSN) (www.csn.com) that will present a wide variety of science programming 24/7. The potential of CSN can be deduced from the news that Wendall Bailey and Reese Schonfeld, two top level veterans of the broadcasting and television industries, have joined the CSN Advisory Board. Wendall Bailey was Vice President for Science and Technology at the National Cable Television Association (NCTA). Reese Schonfeld was founding President and CEO of the Cable News Network (CNN); he was also founding President and CEO of the Food Network.

GNN will be similar to CSN, but much broader in scope. Many people thought Ted Turner was crazy when he set up CNN. GNN will be infinitely more revolutionary and should be just as successful. Instead of television being a cultural desert; new networks like CSN and GNN will trigger a golden age of enlightenment, good will, and morality.

All the giant media companies have piled up mountains of debt by vastly overpaying for acquisitions and expansion, instead of developing better programming. Experts say that for any business to be successful, it must enjoy a unique selling advantage over its competitors. GNN will enjoy an enormous marketing advantage over the competing networks by virtue of the breadth and diversity of its programming (literally infinite) as well as the positive, upbeat, wholesome nature of its product. Not only will GNN appeal to a much wider viewing audience than any of the competing networks, but it will also attract a much broader spectrum of advertisers.

Existing cable news channels repeat essentially the same news every 23 minutes, 24 hours a day. As a result, the average viewer only tunes in once or twice a day to get the news. This greatly limits advertiser exposure opportunity. GNN with its infinitely varied programming, would entice the viewer to tune in more often and stay tuned longer; resulting in greatly enhanced advertiser opportunity.

In the long run, these advantages should make GNN the largest and most profitable network in the television industry. The global appetite for new programming is exploding. With new networks like CSN and GNN the old lament will no longer be true — "there's nothing on TV tonight!"

GOOD NEWS vs NIGHTMARE ALLEY

Instead of watching another beheading or terrorist bombing, wouldn't it be more healthy to watch a test-flight of Burt Rutan's Globalflyer?

Rather than listening to another of Bush vs Kerry poll numbers, why not take a tour of Bill Gates' mansion?

Rather than endure another discussion of the Laci Peterson trial, wouldn't it be much more diverting to visit one of the "high society" balls at the beautiful Breakers Hotel during Palm Beach's "Season."

Wouldn't viewers rather watch the revelers at the Munich "Oktoberfest" than another episode of Roseanne?

Wouldn't most viewers rather take a ride on Bavaria's fabulous "Alpenstrasse" than watch another discussion of Michael Jackson or Kobi Bryant?

Rather than polluting young minds with Howard Stern or Scream, why not watch a classic car like Delage or Talbot Lago being restored by a top restoration shop.

To visualize the financial prospects of such programming, one only need observe how the Fortune 500 corporations compete to buy advertising for good news events like the Bowl games, the World Series, or the Olympics. Researchers at Carnegie Mellon University have found that bad moods brought on by sadness and disgust are bad for business. If sad or disgusting programming directly affects people's willingness to buy advertisers products, happy programming should be very good for business.

THEODORE V. MORRISON, JR.
CHAIRMAN

CLINTON MILLER
COMMISSIONER

MARK C. CHRISTIE
COMMISSIONER

JOEL H. PECK
CLERK OF THE COMMISSION
P.O. BOX 1197
RICHMOND, VIRGINIA 23218-1197

STATE CORPORATION COMMISSION
Office of the Clerk   September 9, 2004

JAMES B EDWARDS
2923 24TH STREET N
ARLINGTON, VA 22207

RE: Good News Network, Inc.
ID: - 0
DCN: 04-09-08-0055

Dear Customer:

We are returning the articles of incorporation for the following reasons:

The articles cannot be approved because the corporate name is not distinguishable upon our records from a corporation of record whose name is GOOD NEWS NETWORK. It will therefore be necessary for you to select a new name for the proposed corporation, as required by the provisions of Section 13.1-630 of the Code of Virginia for a stock corporation or Section 13.1-829 of the Code for a nonstock corporation.

If you desire to check the availability of a corporate name, please call the Clerk's Office at (804) 371-9733 or toll-free in Virginia at (866) 722-2551.

We have deposited the $75.00 submitted for the filing of this document and will credit it to the required fees when the document is returned and filed. Please note that, unless the document is resubmitted or a refund is requested prior to 12 months after the date of deposit, these funds will be irretrievably forfeited to the Treasurer of Virginia.

NOTE: Return this letter with your resubmission of all required document(s) to ensure prompt processing and proper crediting of fees.

Sincerely,

Jana P. Leonard
Attorney
(804) 225-8524

NEWCREJ
CIS0378

Tyler Building, 1300 East Main Street, Richmond, VA 23219-3630
Clerk's Office (804) 371-9733 or (866) 722-2551 (toll-free in Virginia) www.state.va.us/scc/division/clk
Telecommunications Device for the Deaf-TDD/Voice: (804) 371-9206

COMMONWEALTH OF VIRGINIA

CLINTON MILLER
CHAIRMAN

MARK C. CHRISTIE
COMMISSIONER

THEODORE V. MORRISON, JR.
COMMISSIONER

JOEL H. PECK
CLERK OF THE COMMISSION
P.O. BOX 1197
RICHMOND, VIRGINIA 23218-1197

STATE CORPORATION COMMISSION
Office of the Clerk   July 21, 2005

JAMES B EDWARDS
2923 24TH STREET N
ARLINGTON, VA 22207-0000

RE: Good News Television, Inc.
ID: 0623799 - 4
DCN: 205550602

Dear Customer:

The enclosed Annual Report is returned for the reason(s) indicated as follows:

All directors and principal officers must be listed in item 7 of the annual report. One individual may be a director and an officer. See Sections 13.1-675 A and 13.1-693 A or Sections 13.1-855 A and 13.1-872 A of the Code of Virginia. Note: If the corporation (1) does not have directors because (i) initial directors are not named in the articles of incorporation and an organizational meeting of the corporation has not been held or (ii) the board of directors has been eliminated pursuant to a valid shareholder agreement authorized by 13.1-671.1 of the Code of Virginia, or (2) does not have officers because an organizational meeting has not been held, insert "No Directors" or "No Directors and Officers," as the case may be, in the right block in item 7. OFFICER INFORMATION IS MISSING OR INCOMPLETE.

If you have any questions, please call (804) 371-9733 or toll-free in Virginia, 1-866-722-2551.

Sincerely,

Clerk's Office

ARREJECT
CIS0307

Tyler Building, 1300 East Main Street, Richmond, VA 23219-3630
Clerk's Office (804) 371-9733 or (866) 722-2551 (toll-free in Virginia) www.scc.virginia.gov/division/clk
Telecommunications Device for the Deaf-TDD/Voice: (804) 371-9206

Mismatch

James B. Edwards was born 3/21/98 in Emporia, VA. Anna Odessa Hooten was born 7/12/98 at Hooten's Fork in Washington, NC. Both graduated from high school. Mother trained as a nurse at Washington Hospital. In WWI, Dad was a Machinist's Mate on a Navy destroyer. When he got out of the Navy, Uncle Algie got him a job in the Finance Division of the Norfolk Post Office. I don't know how my parents met, but they were married 4/5/24; I was their first anniversary present.

From 1927 to 1930, we lived in a small house out beyond Fairmount Park. One summer day, when I was five years old, I was sitting on the front porch looking at my Jesus book. Sunday School level Christianity was the only form of education imparted to me by my parents. Granny Pat came out to join me. Before she could settle in, I said: "Granny, please go back inside, I'm lonesome enough by myself". She beat a hasty retreat; prolonged guffaws followed from the kitchen.

Like Sisyphus, Mother was always ardently attacking the social ladder. We had to live in a larger house in a "better" neighborhood. Dad had a house built in Winona. Frances E. Willard Elementary and Lafayette Presbyterian were short walks away. Dad taught Sunday School and was very popular with the boys, everybody wanted to be in his class. Dad was "happy in his work" in the Finance Division; he was a good worker and popular. Mother had higher aspirations. Lindsey Warren was Comptroller General of the U.S. Herbert Bonner was U.S. Congressman from Washington, NC. Mother had known both of them all of her life, they grew up a few blocks apart. Her brother Preston was in the same platoon with Bonner in WWI. Mother conducted periodic pilgrimages to DC to see Warren and Bonner. She was crusading to have Dad promoted to Postmaster. This was mission impossible; the job was a highly sought political plum. Mother was undeterred; logic and reason were undiscovered territories. Dad had always been well-liked by management. Now he became and "eminence gris"; someone to be watched.

One summer afternoon the neighborhood kids were having boxing matches in Tubby Lindblad's backyard. Tubby's father, Dad and Mr. Outten, our next door neighbor, were watching. Mr. Outten and Dad matched Welly Outten and I. I was nine, Welly was ten and larger; I won. The Loebsack boys were the toughest kids in the neighborhood. Dad matched me with Richard Loebsack, who was about my size, but twelve years old. Richard knocked me out. My father "the matchmaker". Mr. Outten hired Richard to give Welly boxing lessons – it was a turning point - Welly became strong and self-confident. Richard was not hired to train me. What I really needed in life was a mentor. My father was not a mentor; he never really liked me.

My parents were a disastrous mismatch. She was discontented and a spendthrift. He was contented and frugal. Dad would have a drink with you; Mom was a Carrie Nation. Our house was furnished with only the finest. Carfare tokens were three for a quarter; Dad often walked three miles from work to save a token. He repaired our shoes with half-soles, which would come loose and flap. If Dad came home with any trace of "demon rum"; Mom would go ballistic. Sometimes she wouldn't let him in the house, even if it was snowing. Sometimes he would sleep in the garage in the car. While I was overseas, they broke up. It was very hard on my brother who was thirteen. Dad was living in a rented room downtown. This was devastating for him; at heart he was a homebody.

While B Company was working the St.Vith area in February 1945, I received some "interesting" mail. A letter from Granddad told me Granny had died of cancer. A letter from Lindsey Warren reported Mother had seen him about how I was being mistreated by the Army. I had no idea what in the world was going on; I was being treated like everybody else. My Company CO came to ask me if I was alright. All I could say was: "It's my Mother". That same month , I got a letter from Mother telling me she and Dad had split.

If Mother had been normal our family would have lived out "the American dream". Dad would have savored a couple of drinks, had dinner, listened to the radio and gone to bed. Dad would have moved up by seniority to Chief Clerk of the Finance Division. Mother always wanted to live in Larchmont; I'm sure her badgering would have gotten us there.

"Of all sad tales of tongue and pen; the saddest of all – it might have been".

Alas, "the American dream" became "the American tragedy". Dad's dispair drove him to heavier drinking, even on the job. Mother worked as a nurse in one of the hospitals or nursing homes, but she still hounded Dad for financial support. Dad was demoted to the mail room floor, putting-up mail in the PO boxes. While all this transpired I was away at UVA. One afternoon, I came across and an article in a Norfolk paper about the Court finding a postal clerk, James B. Edwards, guilty of theft and sentencing him to one year in the Federal Correctional Facility in Richmond. In impoverished desperation, he had taken money, usually dollar bills from the envelopes of a Charity. His total "haul" was under $40.

Everyone but me knew about it. Strangely I was not greatly distressed by this; nothing in the war really troubled me either. God had provided me with protective armor. In a crisis or tragedy, I went into a detached state. This is strange, because I'm hyper-empathetic. I can feel the cold with the Zeks in the Gulag or the pain of the torture victim in Sukhanovka.

My graduation was on hold due to an incomplete in Chemistry Lab at W&M/VPI. The UVA administrators knew about my Dad. My graduation was up to the Registrar, Dr Ferguson. The good doctor had a "drinking problem". He sometimes conducted his classes at the Virginia, a bar at "the Corner". As a fellow alki, I'm sure he empathized with my Dad. At our meeting in the Rotunda, I said: "Under the circumstances, Doctor, don't you think the University would do well to get rid of people like me as soon as possible?" He said: "Maybe you're right, Edwards". God bless Dr Ferguson.

Dad didn't like me while I was growing up. When I was grown and started marrying and squiring beautiful women, he changed his appraisal

– he always had an "eye for the ladies". He died of emphysema in 1966 while I was running Gunfighter – he was 68. Mother died in 1998 after falling and fracturing her skull – she was 100. Until her fall, she was still as "strong as an ox". She and Bonner and Warren are buried near each other in Oakdale Cemetery, near where they grew up.

Granny

My grandmother, Emily Hubbard Edwards was my favorite relative. She was the only one who understood me. Understood that I was a good little boy, who never needed punishing, who just needed to be left alone to do his own thing. His own thing was elaborate day dreaming – exciting adventures in which he was the hero. I don't recall her ever correcting me over anything – I gave her no cause.

I spent several weeks every summer at my grandparents home at 441 South Main Street, Emporia, VA. A large wooden two-story house with two bedrooms downstairs and three up. The three upstairs bedrooms had belonged to their sons – Algie, James and Roscoe (Pete). My Dad and Pete's rooms they rented out. Algie, the eldest, smartest, handsomest, nicest, they kept vacant, as he had left it; he had been tragically murdered when I was seven. Algie was the only member of my family on either side who had a library, mostly classics like Babbitt and Vanity Fair. The first real book I ever read was his book on the sinking of the Titanic. Algie took me every Saturday to the Bird Theater in Norfolk to see a cowboy movie and buy me a bag of roasted peanuts. His manner and smile were magic.

Grandad, Thomas Hartwell Edwards, was about five foot, five inches tall, hair parted in the middle, Buster Keaton style; a great handlebar mustache. He ran a crew of lumberjacks for a sawmill near town. Every Saturday he got a shave and a haircut at the corner barbershop. One Saturday, I saw him beat up three young large lumberjacks who called him a liar.

The house fronted on Main Street and backed up to the Southern Railroad tracks, on a 75 foot by 150 foot lot. Half the backyard was a chicken yard the other half a vegetable garden. The chicken yard ended at the garage, hen house, woodhouse, and a large Black Walnut tree. The garden had every kind of vegetable, the woodhouse was full of barked, pine scraps used to fuel the kitchen and room stoves. Every morning,

Granny fired up the cast-iron stove and made a batch of clabber biscuits – they were the best I've ever eaten. She would stuff pine sticks into the firebox, pour some kerosene from a little tin pitcher and light with a strike-anywhere match. She mixed the dough in a large, oblong, hand-carved wooden bowl with a leather tong so it could be hung on the wall. Today, it sits a top the commode in my living room. The biscuits were served with a slab of butter and Granny's homemade preserves – pear, grape, or strawberry. I would sit in rapt silent attention through the whole operation. Often, neither of us spoke. Her every move was as precise and unerring as a robot.

Sometimes, I would ask questions. Having a religious orientation, one morning I asked her: "Granny, what do you think of Billy Sunday?" Her reply: "Don't like him." "Why?" I inquired. Granny: "He told the women in the congregation to cross their legs and shut the gates of hell".

She was a pioneer of the KISS system (Keep It Simple Stupid). She and Granddad had a silver Iver-Johnson .32 caliber revolver. One day I asked her to show me how to use it. We took it out on the back porch. She showed me how to aim and squeeze off shots. She fired a shot into the old rain barrel by the woodshed and handed the gun to me. I fired a couple of shots and we put the gun back in the pantry. It was the same when she taught me how to drive. She drove the Model A Ford to a dirt horse track outside town. She showed me how to use the gears, clutch and gas. She put me behind the wheel and said: "Drive JB". I drove around the track for about twenty minutes. I was eleven; that's the only driving lesson I ever had.

There was a row of big wooden rocking chairs on the front porch. Granny and I would sit rocking while we shucked corn and shelled peas and butter beans we had just picked in the garden. Town ladies in their cotton frocks and broad brimmed hats would stop to chat with Granny. Sometimes, we sat in the swing and counted Fords and Chevy s – a contest. Some afternoons we'd walk a few block down Main to the Theater to see a Western. She would add to the festivities by buying a pack of Beemans Chewing Gum. Chuck Yaeger always relied on Beemans.

In World War I, Algie was in the Army, Dad was on a Destroyer in the Navy. After the war, Algie got a job in the Finance Division of the Norfolk Post office; he got Dad a job in the same office. The shared an apartment on Mobray Arch, most of which was owned by an uncle named Robert Hogue. I have pictures of Dad and Uncle Algie taken on the waterfront of Mobray Arch. As handsome and dapper as leading men, clad in Brooks Brothers suits, Chesterfields, and Fedoras. Granny and Granddad never got over the loss of Algie. Granny thought I was like Algie. I wrote to her regularly while I was in the Army. During the Battle of the Bulge, I got a letter from Granddad telling me she had died. Someone irreplaceable went out of my life; most days I think of her.

The Fabulous Fifties

The Fifties – America's Golden Age.
The Age of the WWII veterans "The Greatest Generation".
The Age of Prosperity and Hope.
The Age of Romance – Love was sweeping the country.
The Age of High Fidelity and Classical Music.
The Golden Age of Musicals:
The Sound of Music, My Fair Lady, Guys and Dolls, The Music Man, The King and I, West Side Story, Damn Yankees, Call Me Madam, Can-Can.

Nearly everyone you worked with was a veteran – most had "seen the elephant" (been in combat). They were mature; ambitious ; "ready, willing and able"; the men in the "Grey Flannel Suits". Lovers of America.

High-fidelity systems and classical music were the rage. The music we hum inside our head shapes our soul. Everybody competed to have the latest equipment and the newest Berlioz or Beethoven. I had a corner Klipsch Horn with a 16-inch woofer, a midrange horn, and a tweeter, all powered by a huge amplifier – it would peel the wallpaper. Everybody "made out". Dates were "SOP". Dinner, or a club, or a play, or a movie; back to your place or hers; Beethoven, Bubbly, and Bed. I matriculated a galaxy of lovelies to Gilbert & Sullivan. When my brother came home from Korea in 1954, he was hep on R&B, so he and I toured the bars in NE and SE DC. We were usually the only "whiteys" in the place; nobody messed with us. If you want a short cut to the Obituaries try going into a bar in NE or SE DC today. The DC area was filled with used book stores. The 1700 block of Pennsylvania Avenue, one block from the White House, was lined on both sides with multi-story row houses that were used book stores. Several blocks of 9th Street, NW were also lined on both sides with more used book stores. There were large stores in Alexandria and Bethesda. None exist today. All the above ended with the Hippie Generation in the 1960s.

These people did not love America. There was a tsunami-scale decline in American culture.

The Ladies

Let me start by saying every woman I was married to or seriously involved with was a lovely, fantastic, wonderful woman. They were beautiful, intelligent, witty, fun, and great lovers – ready any time, anyplace. Many men are compelled to make byzantine advanced arrangements for sex – I never encountered this vexation.

First there was Cathrine Juanita Beamon (Johnnie) a pretty little blond, self-described as: "five feet two and a little piece". We met through my Army buddy Johnny Barlow's girlfriend, Ann Rivers. I took her to her high-school graduation prom. We were married when I transferred to UVA in the Fall of 1948. We rented a room in a lovely home in Fry Springs. The owner was the widow of United Fruit Co. executive, accustomed to the good life; the bed sheets were silk. Four male students also bunked there. About two weeks after we arrived, the widow called me into her office to tell me we would have to leave. She said Johnnie was having an affair with one of the guys. I already had my suspicious. One day I came home early, and heard tiny footsteps racing down the hall to our room. At the top of the stairs, I noticed one of the guys intently reading in a wing back chair. Johnnie was in bed wearing a pink baby doll, the covers pulled up to her chin and looking like the cat who just swallowed the canary. Something deep down inside died.

Next stop on La Ronde was the Scotts. The Scotts rented out a basement apartment to students. Mr Scott was a practicing seducer. While I was attending classes, Scott was attending Johnnie. We were rescued by Copeley Hill. Copeley Hill was a large trailer park, owned by the University, where most of the married students lived. Copeley Hill was fun; like the rest of the University, every weekend was Party, Party, Party. After graduation Johnnie went back to Longwood, I went to San Diego. Johnnie was a wonderful little girl – passionate, loving, witty, fun, sensible, pragmatic – I never saw her lose her temper or her cool. She was, however, more than somewhat "fidelity challenged".

Ruth M. Roche was from Boston – intelligent, witty, funny, well-read, great ballerina legs. Ruth had been Justice Robert Jackson's secretary at the Nuremberg Trials. She was on General Curtis Le May's staff at the Pentagon. We met at a Hi-Fi party, where the host had just bought a huge, powerful, expensive system. Ruth invited me to her place to hear her system. I introduced her to G&S. She was instantly addicted and soon owned every operetta, she passionately extolled each new acquisition. She introduced me to the Saturday Review of Literature, which we read together cover to cover.

As I mentioned the 1700 block of Pennsylvania Avenue was lined with used book emporiums. It was also the home of two of Washington's best restaurants. Jack Hunt's Seafood (northside) and Arnold's Hofbrauhaus (southside) directly opposite each other in the middle of the block. Both offered excellent food at good prices. Being a half-block from the White House and EOB, meant their clientèle were usually interesting. Ruth and I often dined at one of them and sometimes visited one of the used-book stores afterward. The owners usually lived on the top floor of the store and often threw exotic parties. Ruth went home to Boston to be secretary to W. R. Grace.

Jane Dalgleish Perley went to work at AP&R as Milton Lyons' secretary. I think the Investment Advisory Department managed some of the Dalgleish fortune. She had classic "ruling-class" looks: high-forehead, wide-set eyes, good bone structure, perfect teeth – a Jackie Kennedy type. Her parents and grandmother Dalgleish lived in Spring Valley – the grandmother in a palace. Her father, Frank Perley, was chief of the Office of Legislative Counsel of the House of Representatives. He and Joe Kennedy had written the 1934 Securities and Exchange Act. Around the office, Jane badgered me, it didn't bother me, I ignored her. I didn't realize this was her way of flirting. Finally, at Christmas party, Milton pulled me aside and said: "Why don't you give the kid a break; she nuts about you". Shortly thereafter, we departed for my place. In May, I went to work for Fidelity and was on the road most of the time. Jane and I went together fairly regularly, but not exclusively. After the Fidelity Christmas disaster, I'm afraid I grabbed out like the drowning man and asked Jane to marry me. Neither of us were very enthusiastic, but we went ahead anyway. Jane brought me a large rock with instructions to have if mounted at Galt's Jewelers. She said her mother had taken it from a safety-deposit box full of diamonds at Riggs Bank. I had several offers in wholesaling, but Jane didn't want me to be away on the road. I went to work as a Classifier for the DC Government. It was a poor choice, the office was buried in conflict and intrigue. Jane's mother got her a job at the Carnegie Institute. Jane and I got along well together, we never fought, sex wasn't a problem. Jane was a sweet girl, but reserved, almost taciturn; the antithesis of a raconteur. I think both of us had become depressed and bored. Her family saw me as a loser; the marriage as a mistake – time to cut their losses. One day when Jane stayed home with a cold, her mother came by and took her home – she never returned. Soon after we parted ways, I became wholesaler for National Securities.

Vicki – lovely, delightful, hilarious!
Soon after we were married, Commonwealth Funds hired me as their wholesaler for the TX, OK, LA territory. One Sunday morning soon after we moved to Dallas, I asked Vicki what she wanted to do that day. At this point her English was somewhat fractured. "Lookit Hice" she replied. "What's Hice?" I inquired. "Mouse, Mice; House, Hice – no eh?" My duties as a wholesaler compelled frequent visits to New Orleans, where one is exposed to the likes of Brennan's, Galatoire's, Preservation Hall, the French Antique Shop, Hurricanes, and Boston Club Punch. The people in the securities business in Nawlens exuded a charming antebellum gentility. We bought some lovely Louis XVI pieces at the French Antique Shop. Alas, Commonwealth sold out to American Express and closed the territory. We moved back to DC. I went to work for NASA; Vicki joined Varig. She became assistant manager and unofficial social secretary of Brasil. We traveled often to Europe and Brasil; usually first-class. First-class on Varig meant Beluga caviar and Dom Perignon.

M. Patton Echols Jr

Pat was an Army brat, born in Schofield Barracks (where From Here to Eternity was filmed) in Hawaii in 1925. While his father was stationed at West Point in 1934, Pat watched Flirtation Walk being filmed. His father was on General MacArthur's staff in World War II. Pat graduated from VMI in 1945. He was an Engineer officer in Korea in 1951-52. He got a law degree from George Washington University in 1958, and began practicing in Arlington.

We rented our house at 2923 North 24th Street from Henrietta Baer in 1966. Pat handled the legal work; he lived in the next block at 2814. Ms. Baer had been a silent film star, working out of Mamaronick, NY. Anne Sulkie lived next door at 2921,she had been an editor of the New York Times in the "roaring twenties". Back then, there were no "quotas" or "affirmative action", she was just very good. Her husband was head of the Drama Department at Georgetown University. Next door, at 2917, lived Frances Cruiser, a retired CIA agent, who spoke several Middle Eastern languages. Three very smart women. Miss Baer rented out several houses in Arlington and in the posh Kalorama section of DC. Pat Echols handled all the ladies legal work, and I said he lived in the next block.

Pat was very active in Republican politics. He served a term as a State Senator and ran for Attorney General of Virginia in 1973. He should have won, but was betrayed by some behind the scenes "dirty pool". I met Pat via Henrietta Baer and his daughter Carter Echols, who was our "paper boy"; she wore her hair under a baseball cap. One day when she came to collect she was unmasked, I said: "You're a little girl", she blushed like a rose. Carter became a lay minister and ran the Samaritan Inn in DC for years. The Samaritans rehabilitated the homeless.

Pat and I became good friends because we both loved Gilbert and Sullivan. Pat was president of the Washington Savoyards. I sometimes helped him film their productions. We periodically attended G&S

shows around town. One year, Doyle Carte staged a fantastic review at the Kennedy Center. Their rendition of "When I go out the door" from Patience brought a standing ovation and multiple encores. Pat was also president of the Arlington Optimist Club and often invited me to their luncheons. As guest speaker, I presented my book "Hitler: Stalin's Stooge" at one of the luncheons. Pat was president of the Arlington Commodore Club, where the dandy little Commodore 64 introduced many to the world of computers.

Pat was a Prince. He always stood ready to help out with a problem. His office was in a little white bungalow across the street from the Courthouse, where everyone knew him. He seemed to know every body in Arlington. At home, he had a grand piano in the living room. He usually played classics, operetta, or G&S. I sometimes dropped by his music salon for sundowners and sonatas.

Pat's health went into a rapid decline; he shrank to about three-quarter scale. Vicki and I went by to see him the day before he died. We sat holding hands and singing "Only a Rose". His voice was very weak, but he wanted to sing it again and again. He died that night; he was 86. His funeral was SRO; everyone loved Pat.

E Todo Mundo Vae A Praia

A lot has been left out. I could have written a book about the galaxy of delightful women who bespangled my odyssey with infinite "moments of beauty." Myriad fascinating people and projects were not covered. For example, I worked for three "think-tanks": Cerberus, Galaxy, and AOT. One assignment involved the Mossad, which branded me forever a "person of interest" to German intelligence. Thereafter, on any trip to Germany, at some point, a gorgeous little blonde "Erika" type would manage to join me at lunch or dinner and ask a lot of friendly questions about my trip. German intelligence knew my type: "five-foot-two", blonde, ballerina legs.

After Gunfighter, Jay Carsey hired me as Assistant to the President for New Projects. We planned to set up a polymathic accelerated education course in which students would receive an across-the-board introduction to the major disciplines: biology, chemistry, economics, engineering, history, physics, etc. An introduction to the available options of academe. We were putting together funding when Jay made his dramatic exit. We often joked about doing a Zorba dance if our world crashed. Alas, we never did.

I believe in miracles and devine intervention. There were many instances I know about; I'm sure there were many I did not. Some, involving women, I'm not going to discuss. In Fayes-Les-Veneurs, on the morning of 1/17/45, B Company trucks were departing for jobs; my squad truck was loaded except for me. Platoon sergeant Rainus appeared: "Eddie, they need a man in the kitchen". I said: "Why me?" Rainus: "Because you're the only guy in the street". Later in the day our truck ran over an anti-tank (AT) mine, wounding most of the squad. On a Spring day in 1945, I went to Seashore State Park for a swim. Despite being a lousy swimmer, I was exuberantly swimming straight out to sea. Suddenly, my hand crashed into something very large. Shark! Christ walked on the waters of Gallilee; I ran on the waters of Seashore State Park! Later, I learned porpoises feel like a woman's thigh. God had sent one of his lovely porpoises to save me from a watery grave.

A general observation on life. You can't go too far astray if you try
to live by the Gospel of St. Matthew (chapters 5-7), Kipling's If, and
The Boy Scout Handbook. Americans end stories with: "and they lived
happily ever after".

Brasilians say: "E todo mundo vae a praia". "and everybody went to
the beach".

Other books by the author:

The Great Technology Race (1993)
The nations that will lead the world of the future are those which develop and control the new technologies, such as: Artificial Intelligence, Nanotechnology, Photonics, Supercomputers, Superconductivity.

Hitler: Stalin's Stooge (2004)
Hitler was the stooge Stalin used to start World War II. Stalin was the "eminence gris" behind the rise of Hitler and the Nazis to power. Stalin envisioned World War II as a replay of World War I, in which the Europeans would destroy each other and be ripe for conquest. Stalin forged the mightiest political control apparatus and the largest military machine in the world. In the process, tens of millions were executed or perished in the vast Gulag. Utopia Empowered became Murder Incorporated ! Stalin planned to use this nightmare mechanism to conquer and control a war-ravaged Europe. Hitler preempted him by two weeks.

There is a Silver Bullet (2007)
Set America Free (SAF)says we can have total energy independence in four years. SAF says 50% of U.S. cars are driven 20 miles per day or fewer. A plug-in hybrid vehicle (PHEV) with a 20-mile electric only range would reduce U.S. fuel consumption by 85%. Gas-guzzlers can be replaced by 100mpg PHEVs. Fifty million acres of switchgrass could produce enough ethanol to meet all of our fuel requirements.

Silver Bullets II (2010)
In the past 150 years (since 1859), the entire world has consumed one trillion barrels of oil. America has two trillion barrels of residual oil in 400,000 capped-off oil wells. Beneath the Rocky Mountains, in the vast Bakken Formation, America has two trillion barrels of light, sweet crude oil.

The Canadian tar sands contain over two trillion barrels of oil. America has 275 billion tons of coal, enough to last 300 years; convertible to trillions of barrels of oil. There are over 1700 1000 megawatt coal-fired power plants in the U.S. that could produce 170 billion gallons of bio-fuel per year if equipped with algae bio-reactors to capture CO_2 emissions. Fifty million acres of switchgrass could produce over 140 billion gallons of ethanol per year.

Something Unexpected and Terrible (2012)
The South is secretly building a superbattleship in Europe to smash the Union blockade and lay waste to Northern port cities. Union spies fan out across Europe to track down the Confederate sea monster. UVA professor, Colby Curtis leads them on a wild goose chase from wartime Richmond to Charles Dicken's London, Gottingen University, Krupp's Gartenhaus, and sunny Napoli. The Union and the Confederacy race to develop new naval and gun technology. There is a frightful massacre off Cape Fear. The climax is a wild shootout of superships in Hampton Roads.

CPSIA information can be obtained
at www.ICGtesting.com
Printed in the USA
FFHW02n1228180918
48332941-52158FF